Learning To
LIVE

Learning To
LIVE

A Ladies' Bible Study

SHAMARION WHITAKER

authorHOUSE®

AuthorHouse™ LLC
1663 Liberty Drive
Bloomington, IN 47403
www.authorhouse.com
Phone: 1-800-839-8640

Published by AuthorHouse 03/07/2014

ISBN: 978-1-4918-6465-4 (sc)
ISBN: 978-1-4918-6489-0 (e)

Introduction

Learning to Live is a book about growing, maturing, and in the process, learning more about who you really are. Every experience you have in life has the purpose of teaching you something about yourself. No doubt, you've been a student during your lifetime; whether it was in elementary school, junior high, high school, or perhaps even in college. In a classroom, there's an instructor. Learning takes place. Think of life as a huge classroom where experiences are your instructor.

Unfortunately, experiences that teach us the most are those that are painful and challenging, those that leave us emotionally and mentally battered, wounded and scarred. But nevertheless, learning more about who you are requires spending time in life's classroom even when it's painful and uncomfortable.

Why is it necessary to learn more about who you are? Learning more about yourself reveals those things you need to change. If they're never revealed, you may never change. I always thought I was confident and sure of myself until life presented me with an experience that revealed my insecurities. I thought I was a forgiving person until I experienced being deeply hurt by someone I struggled to forgive. I thought I was selfless in my actions and deeds until life presented me with an experience that revealed my selfish nature. I thought I knew how to love unconditionally until life handed me an experience that revealed a lack of love.

Learning to Live will share some of life's experiences that are common to many and will help you get to know yourself and perhaps even reveal things that are buried deep within. You're sure to be reminded of experiences you've had, those that brought joy as well as those that brought pain.

What we learn about ourselves is not always pleasant. Experiences not only reveal the good in us, but they also reveal those things we need to put to death and rid ourselves of. King David, a person the Bible refers to as a man after God's own heart, encountered experiences that revealed his flaws and imperfections. He had a sexual encounter with another man's wife, impregnated her, and in his effort to cover it up, he ordered the murder of her husband (2 Samuel 11:2-15).

The experiences we encounter in life's classroom don't always work in us what God intends. The Lord expects our experiences to change us and make us more like the image of His Son. The Bible teaches, *"But we all, with unveiled face, beholding as in a mirror the glory of the Lord, are being transformed into the same image from glory to glory, just as by the Spirit of the Lord"* (2 Corinthians 3:18). He expects our experiences to point us to a higher good, to change our focus from earth to heaven. *"Therefore we do not lose heart. Even though our outward man is perishing, yet the inward man is being renewed day by day. For our light affliction, which is but for a moment, is working for us a far more exceeding and eternal weight of glory"* (2 Corinthians 4:16-17).

As life's experiences reveal those things about you that don't line up with the Word of God and His will, the opportunity for you to change or be transformed is always there. Transformation isn't always easy, nor is it always pleasant. And even though many of life's experiences come in the form of challenges that are difficult to overcome, every experience has a lesson, and through every experience, you should ask, "Lord, what do you want me to learn from this experience?"

In order for the experiences you encounter in life to work in you and teach you more about yourself, provoking transformation in your life, you have to be open to learn. You need an open and receptive mind that's conducive to learning. If you're not open and receptive to learning, to changing and becoming better than you are, you may never learn the lessons life wants to teach you.

As you read this book, it will provoke self-examination as I share biblical, foundational principles that will help you in your efforts to change those things you need to change in order to line up with the will and purpose of God. And while it's a book about change and transformation, it's also about making mistakes.

Mistakes are an integral part of life. You will find that in your mistakes, in your disappointments, in your fears and in your tears; this is where you experience the personal and spiritual growth necessary for true transformation, that you might reclaim the life you were meant to live.

As you read and study the principles shared, you are sure to recall those experiences in your past that helped to shape and define your life. As I share my experiences and the foundational principles that have guided my path, you may recall moments that remind you of the lessons you've learned in life, things you've learned about yourself, revealed through life's experiences. As you recall those defining moments, I pray that you will evaluate the thoughts and emotions connected to those memories, explore the principles offered in this book, and use them to release, renew and rebuild your life.

The lessons taught by life's experiences; embrace them, welcome them and learn from them, even those that are uncomfortable and unpleasant. Make the principles taught in *Learning to Live* part of your life. Allow them to work in you as you become the person God created you to be.

Table of Contents

Chapter 1

Understand Your Weaknesses

"The Contest"

"For we do not have a High Priest
who cannot sympathize with our weaknesses,
but was in all points tempted as we are,
yet without sin" (Hebrews 4:15).

One afternoon in one of my seventh grade classes, our teacher was reading poetry to the class. When she finished reading and lecturing, she selected a verse from one of the poems she had read. Then she gave instructions to the class. Her instructions were for each student, one at a time, to raise their voice and read the verse out loud to their peers. Some of the students read the poetic verse with feeling and emotion, while others simply read with no emotional expression at all. Finally, it was my turn. I read the verse and then took my seat.

When the last student finished reading, the teacher asked us to take out a piece of paper and pencil. She asked each student to write down the name of the student they felt demonstrated the most talent in reading the verse of poetry. She informed us that this was a contest to determine who would go on to participate in an upcoming literary competition.

When the votes were tallied and the winner announced, I was speechless and totally surprised to find out I had won the competition. I thought, "You mean I won?" It was difficult to believe my peers chose me. In fact, it actually made me feel uncomfortable. I didn't feel as though I deserved to win. I didn't think I was all that good.

The Power of Low Self-Esteem

Feelings of not being good enough are common when you don't realize your value and worth. As I look back over my childhood, I see a mental picture of a little girl longing to be like other girls. I was never pretty enough, never good enough, always wanting to fit in. I was never satisfied with just being me.

When I was in junior high school, I remember listening to girls engage in conversations that were of a sexual nature. I wanted to be like them. I felt that perhaps if I were more like them, I would be more popular, more accepted. My older sister, who was in high school, would invite friends to our house and many of them were male. One of the guys who came over always found the perfect opportunity to touch me inappropriately. Instead of seeing this for what it was, I felt acceptance. I was flattered that someone actually found me attractive.

I had always been a good student academically, especially in elementary school. However, by the time I got to seventh grade, school was a lot more challenging and the A's were much more difficult to achieve. But one thing was for sure. Being a straight A student was a good accomplishment, but it just wasn't enough to raise my self-esteem and help me realize I had value and worth.

Self-esteem challenges in elementary and junior high school became an even greater issue as I grew into high school age. These challenges became stronger and had greater control over my life, to the point that when I graduated from high school, I was a single mother.

Characteristics of Weaknesses

Low self-esteem has a serious impact on the lives of many women, and for this reason, it's necessary to evaluate and understand the basis of such.

Perhaps you've fought your own battles with self-esteem, and like many others, the root cause of your challenges can be found in childhood. If you were teased and made to feel unattractive as a child, verbally abused and told you would never amount to anything, physically abused and made to feel your life didn't matter, you likely developed scars and wounds. Unfortunately, the mental and emotional challenges you suffer as a child can certainly determine the quality of your personal and social life as an adult. A scar or wound from childhood can become the weakness that challenges you in your adult life.

Weaknesses make you feel flawed, inadequate and not good enough. And while you may not suffer from emotional scars and wounds that happened in childhood, chances are, your life includes weaknesses. Every person's life has its share of weaknesses. In fact, for every strength you were blessed with, it's balanced by a flaw or weakness.

Unfortunately, instead of focusing on our strengths, it's our weaknesses that are commonly the focus of our attention. Even in childhood, we were conditioned to focus more on what's wrong with us than what's right. If your child brings home a report card that shows they made all A's and one F, which grade will garner the most attention? For sure, the subject that will receive the greatest attention will be the grade that's weakest.

A weakness has certain characteristics. It can be something false and has no basis, or it can be something that's genuine and real, such as an obvious handicap, which may be revealed in a wheelchair, a walker, or something else that makes a handicap obvious. A weakness can be of a mental, emotional, or social nature, even of a spiritual nature, and therefore, may not be so obvious. Another characteristic of a weakness is, it's something you don't seem to have control over. Instead, weaknesses have power over you and can totally control your thoughts and actions. They can stifle you and keep you from exercising your strengths. A weakness can put you at a disadvantage. It can become a "thorn" in your side, an obstacle in your life.

Weaknesses can show up in different areas of life. Your weakness may be an illness you were diagnosed with that makes you feel inadequate. It may be an addiction. We usually think of addictions as those that are drug or alcohol related. Sometimes this is the case. In fact, an addiction to prescription drugs seems to be a common addiction in our day and time. But it's not always alcohol or drugs. There are a number of things you can develop an addiction to, including those of a sexual nature such as an addiction to pornography. Certain foods can be addictive such as sweets. The fact of the matter is, any substance you allow yourself to engage in excessively, with no regard for the potential for harm, is an abuse of the substance, and those who abuse substances in such a way are addicts.

Another weakness you may struggle with is a questionable past. There's a part of your life you feel would be better off left in the past. Skeletons that have been in the closet for years threaten to reveal themselves. In fact, persons closest to you, your family and friends, may not even know about your past life.

These are just a few of the weaknesses individuals struggle with. And for many, this struggle takes place on a daily basis.

You may be asking questions like, "Why does life have to include weaknesses?" "Why can't I live a life of freedom, a life that's free from weaknesses?" "Why do I have to live with the burden of this illness?" "Why can't I overcome my drug addiction?" "Why does the trauma of my past keep haunting me?" "Why can't I just be free?"

Don't beat yourself up over your weaknesses. God knows about the challenges you're experiencing. He's aware of the "thorn" in your side. And even with all of your flaws and imperfections, He still loves you.

According to the Bible, God uses imperfect people. Moses was chosen by God to lead His people out of Egyptian slavery. Moses said, *"Oh, my Lord, I am not eloquent, neither before nor since You have spoken to Your servant; but I am slow of speech and slow of tongue"* (Exodus 4:10). Moses quickly pointed out his weaknesses to God. "I am slow of speech and slow of tongue." I wonder if Moses meant something like this. "Public speaking? Oh, that's my weakness. I'm not strong in that area. People will notice this as soon as I open my mouth. I'm concerned about what people will think about me when they hear me speak. I don't speak eloquently. That's just not me. In fact, sometimes it takes me a long time to say what I have to say because I have to think before I speak, and people might misunderstand and think I'm just slow."

By the power of God, Moses went on to do what he was chosen to do. The message to you is, when the Lord gives you something to do, focus on your strengths and not on your weaknesses.

Fear and Weaknesses

One of the most common elements of weaknesses is fear; a fear of others finding out about your weakness. Keeping your weakness a secret can become a fulltime job, can cause mental and emotional stress, and can make your weakness seem a lot larger than it really is. You'll find yourself expending a huge amount of effort and energy to keep your weakness from being exposed.

Why the secrecy? There are several reasons you may go to great lengths to hide your weakness. First of all, you may be concerned about what others will think of you if your weakness is revealed, concerned about how they will perceive you. You may think that if your weakness is revealed, it will have a devaluing effect, and the perception others have of you will immediately change. You may have a fear of being judged and misunderstood by others. These may be some of the reasons you attempt to wear a mask that conceals your weakness, making it easier for you to continue showing others a side of you that says, "I have it all together. Weaknesses? What weaknesses?"

Pride and Weaknesses

There's another important element of weaknesses that warrants consideration. Be careful to make sure your efforts to keep your weakness secret are not developed out of pride. A person who will go to great lengths to keep their weakness hidden from others could be the same person who is lifted up in pride. When a spirit of pride comes to visit you, and you engage it and allow it to take up space in your life, pride will overcome you and will reflect itself in the perception you have of yourself. When pride becomes a part of you, it reveals an attitude or a spirit that says, "I think very highly of myself, and others think highly of me, too. If I want to continue to have this perception of myself, and if I want others to continue to think highly of me, I need to keep them from finding out about my weakness. I need to keep them from finding out about my flaw. If they find out, I'm doomed. There goes my cover. They will then know that I'm not perfect!"

A person who is controlled by pride will engage in destructive behavior to keep their weakness from being exposed. *"Pride goes before destruction, and a haughty spirit before a fall"* (Proverbs

16:18). They will do just about anything, including jeopardizing their character.

Accept Your Weaknesses

Accepting your weaknesses may seem like a contradiction. You may ask, "Why on earth should I accept something that's such a burden?" Recognize that there are some weaknesses that don't have to remain weaknesses. If there's something about you that puts you at a disadvantage, that causes you to feel inadequate and insecure, something you consider a weakness, by all means, if you can change it, do so. If you're struggling with an issue of a sinful nature, such as an addiction, or if some other form of sin has control of you, partner with the Holy Spirit, your Helper, who can give you strength to work through it and overcome it. "*And I will pray the Father, and He will give you another Helper, that He may abide with you forever*" (John 14:16). God can't use you when you're controlled by sin. Seek to change those things you have the power to change. But remember, life will always issue out weaknesses you don't have the power to change, those you will have to accept and make peace with.

In acceptance, something powerful takes place. A spiritual transformation is at work in you when you decide to make peace with your weakness, your handicap, your illness, or whatever it is you don't have the power to change. In acceptance, the Holy Spirit works in you. Your spiritual vision and perception become clearer. God won't always reveal to you what He's doing in your life, and He doesn't have to. Just know that you were created for Him, and not Him for you. "*For we are His workmanship, created in Christ Jesus for good works, which God prepared beforehand that we should walk in them*" (Ephesians 2:10).

Although God doesn't always reveal what He's specifically doing in your life when He allows weaknesses, it could be the case that He wants to keep you from exalting yourself, or thinking more highly of yourself than you are. The apostle Paul said it best. *"A thorn in the flesh was given to me, a messenger of Satan to buffet me, lest I be exalted above measure"* (2 Corinthians 12:7). Just like Paul's weakness, your weakness could also be God's way of putting a "thorn" in your flesh. The Bible goes on to say that Paul asked God to remove this "thorn." *"Concerning this thing I pleaded with the Lord three times that it might depart from me. And He said to me, „My grace is sufficient for you, for My strength is made perfect in weakness.' Therefore most gladly I will rather boast in my infirmities, that the power of Christ may rest upon me"* (2 Corinthians 12:8-9). Paul learned not to lament over his weaknesses, but to glory in them. As you enter into acceptance of your weaknesses, allow these words to sink into your heart. *"My grace is sufficient for you, for My strength is made perfect in weakness."* These words should infuse you with a sense of freedom and contentment. Recognize that your weaknesses are less about you and more about God doing a work in you.

Reveal Your Weaknesses

Once you've accepted your weaknesses, you should feel less of a need to hide or conceal them. Paul said, *"To the weak I became as weak, that I might win the weak. I have become all things to all men, that I might by all means save some"* (1 Corinthians 9:22). I think Paul is saying that you develop more credibility with others when they can relate to you. If you're trying to help someone go through a spiritual transformation, or you're trying to help them remove an obstacle from their life, they may look at you and say, "If I were more like you, maybe I could do it. But forget it. I'm not as good as you." They respond this way because you're only showing them your good side. Therefore, it's difficult for them to relate to you. But when you get real and up close with people, take off the mask and allow them to see your weaknesses, they will see you as more human, more like them and they can better relate to you, and what you say to them will have more credibility. That's the principle offered in Paul's words when he said, "*To the weak I became as weak, that I might win the weak.*" So take off the mask and let others see not just your strengths, but also your weaknesses.

Accepting your weaknesses and revealing them will put you on the path to working through them, and will empower you to grow both spiritually and emotionally. As you struggle with the power of weaknesses, know that weaknesses are a part of life, and they are just as important as your strengths. The Bible teaches that the pages of your life were written before you were even born. "*My frame was not hidden from you when I was made in secret, and skillfully wrought in the lowest parts of the earth. Your eyes saw my substance, being yet unformed. And in your book they all were written, the days fashioned for me when as yet there were none of them*" (Psalm 139:15-16). When the pages of your life were written, they included not just your strengths, but also your flaws and imperfections. They included your weaknesses.

Christ died in weakness. "*He was oppressed and He was afflicted, yet He opened not His mouth; He was led as a lamb to the slaughter, and as a sheep before its shearers is silent, so He opened not His mouth*" (Isaiah 53:7). "*For though He was crucified in weakness, yet He lives by the power of God. For we also are weak in Him, but we shall live with Him by the power of God toward you*" (2 Corinthians 13:4).

Christ was crucified in weakness, but He proved His strength by His resurrection. He rose from the grave never to die again. Therein lies His strength, and therein lies your strength. "*I have been crucified with Christ; it is no longer I who live, but Christ lives in me*" (Galatians 2:20). In the flesh, you will always have weaknesses.

But in Christ, by the power of God's Holy Spirit, your weaknesses become strengths.

God has a plan for your life. He can use you, even with your weaknesses. Just like He didn't allow the weaknesses of Moses to serve as a limitation or an obstacle to His plan and purpose, He won't allow your weaknesses to hinder the accomplishment of His will. However, in order for His will to be accomplished through you, you must strive to live a life that's holy and acceptable to God. Take your focus off your weaknesses and focus on the Lord and His will for your life. Allow God's Spirit to work in you. The Lord knows you're not perfect. Let Him use an imperfect person to accomplish His perfect will!

Recognize Your Strengths

After winning my seventh grade poetry contest, I went on to participate in a literary competition, won awards, went to high school, gave birth to my son, grew, matured and eventually went off to college. But no matter how much I grew, matured and achieved, I recognized that I had emotional scars and wounds that would follow me into adulthood, and the only way to heal and make peace with my weaknesses was to focus on my strengths.

It was around my second, maybe third year in college. It would be the first time I would make a conscious decision to step outside of my comfort zone and allow myself to be vulnerable.

There were about fifteen girls in the pageant competition. I had worked hard to prepare for the event only to find out a few days before the pageant, I was disqualified because I was a single mother.

I remember the day my sponsor shared the news with me. She explained that because it was so close to the event date, the pageant committee had decided to give me three choices. The first choice was to completely drop out of the pageant. My second choice was to participate in the pageant and not be judged. Thirdly, I could participate in the pageant and be judged along with the other contestants with the possibility of winning the crown. However, the question to be answered was, "Would there be consequences if I chose number three and actually won?" My sponsor told me that if I won, according to the pageant committee, I could keep the crown only if no one contested the decision. But, if anyone contested, I would have to give up my crown.

It wasn't difficult to make my decision. I chose to compete in the pageant and be judged along with the other contestants. I understood what my consequences would be if I won.

The night of the pageant, I tried to forget about the circumstances so I could focus on winning the crown. The first scene of the pageant included all of the contestants walking out on stage to introduce themselves to the audience. The pageant had an African theme, so my sponsor had made me a simple dress made out of fabric that looked like it came from Africa. The colors were gold, bright yellow, red and brown. The top part of the dress was fitted and sleeveless, while the bottom was A-shaped and flared. The hemline was just above the knees. She wrapped my legs in white fur. I looked like a real African princess as I walked out on stage in my bare feet! Needless to say, my outfit was a big hit with the audience. To top it all off, my sponsor taught me how to say "good evening" in an African language.

During the question and answer session, I answered my question perfectly. After the talent competition, I had no regrets. I did a dramatic presentation of Maya Angelou's poem, "Still, I Rise." I can still hear myself belting out the words, *"You may write me down in history with your bitter, twisted lies! You may trod me in the very dirt! But still, like dust, I'll rise!"* After I finished reciting the poem, I sang a verse of James Cleveland's gospel hit, "I Don't Feel No Ways Tired."

The moment of truth had finally come. It was time to hear the names of the runners up and winner. One by one, they were called;

fifth runner up, fourth runner up, third runner up and second runner up. As I stood there waiting for the name of the winner to be called, I felt nervous and anxious. I just wanted it all to be over.

I remember getting up the next morning and going to meet my sponsor. When I got there, she had a local newspaper. I held my breath as she opened the paper. There were photos of all of the winners. And while the night had ended with the judges awarding me the crown, unfortunately, it was a short-lived winning moment. When the pageant was over and the lights went out, the decision to award the crown to me was contested by the first runner up's mother. By the time the paper was printed, I was no longer the winner. According to the listing in the local newspaper, I was first runner up.

As I sat there with my sponsor, I thought back to the night before. When my name was called and I was crowned the winner, the emotions of that moment became the basis of a new level of self-confidence, a new level of self-esteem. The decision I made to compete and be judged was based on my need to heal my scars and wounds, make peace with my weaknesses and turn them into strengths. I saw this as my opportunity to once and for all bind up and throw away all of my insecurities, all of my fears, all of those negative emotions and feelings; especially those that said, "You're not good enough."

FOR DISCUSSION

1. Recall a time in your life, childhood or adulthood, when you felt like you didn't deserve something you were blessed with; a special person in your life, or something else of great value. Share your experience as well as what your feelings of unworthiness were based on.

2. While Hebrews 4:15 is a reference to weakness as it relates to temptations, how can we relate this verse of Scripture to our physical, mental and emotional weaknesses?

3. Sometimes, a lack of trust will keep us from revealing our weaknesses to others. We fear they will judge us, or share our personal information with others. Is this a legitimate reason for not revealing our weaknesses? Give reasons for your answer.

4. In 2 Corinthians 12:8-9, Paul pleaded with God to take away his weakness. Examine these and other verses of Scripture in the chapter and explain why weaknesses can actually be a blessing.

5. Explain the meaning of this statement found on page 3: "An emotional scar or wound from childhood can become the weakness that challenges you in your adult life."

6. Read Exodus 4:10. In this passage of Scripture, Moses was hesitant to do what God asked him to do. He went as far as pointing out his weaknesses to God. We sometimes do the same thing when we're asked to step outside of our comfort zone. Instead of focusing on our strengths, we focus on our weaknesses. Focus on your strengths for a minute. Name three of your strengths.

7. Focusing on your weaknesses can be an indication that you are too concerned with what others think about you. This could be a sign of a prideful spirit. If you are keeping an illness a secret, keeping your financial troubles a secret,

keeping your layoff from the job a secret, all because you want to uphold a certain image, you may have allowed pride to overcome you. Find and share Scriptures that teach the consequences of pride, as well as how God sees a prideful spirit. Start with Proverbs 16:5.

8. In the Bible, we see that it was not uncommon for God to use imperfect people. Who were some of the flawed individuals God used and what were their flaws? Give Scriptures. Include Gideon in Judges 6:15.

9. Christ died in weakness (2 Corinthians 13:4). Matthew 26:39 tells us that Christ asked the Father to "let this cup pass from Me." As we know, God did not let the cup pass. His will was done. Share thoughts on Matthew 26:39. What are the messages we get from this?

10. What role does the Holy Spirit play in helping us accept and find freedom and transformation in our weaknesses? See page 8. Also, find other Scriptures in the Bible that teach the Holy Spirit's role in our lives. Start with Romans 8:26.

Chapter 2

Pray About Everything

"Where's My Shoe!"

"Be anxious for nothing, but in everything
by prayer and supplication, with thanksgiving,
let your requests be made known to God" (Philippians 4:6).

My mother had come to town. When she visits, her visit is usually not complete until we do some shopping. I hadn't been out to the new outlet mall in a while, so we decided to take the short ride just outside of town to shop at some of our favorite stores. Our first stop was at a dress shop. I purchased a dress, some casual tops and then decided to do some shoe shopping. I left my mother in the dress shop and told her to meet me in the shoe store next door.

After trying on several pairs of shoes, I decided on a really cute pair of silver strappy sandals. They would look really good with the new dress I'd just purchased. The heels were the perfect height, and they were extremely comfortable.

It was early evening when my mom and I got back to my house. When we got in, I immediately ran upstairs, tried on my new outfits so I could show off my purchases to my husband. Afterwards, I hung up my new clothes and stored my shoes on the shelf in my closet.

A couple of weeks passed before I decided to pull out my new dress and shoes to wear to church. However, I was in for a big surprise. When I got ready to put on my new silver sandals, I pulled the box down from the closet, opened it and to my surprise, there was only one shoe in the box. "Oh well," I thought. "I must have put the other shoe in the wrong box. Where else could it be? I'm sure I tried them on that night when we got back from shopping." After looking around for the shoe, I gave up and put on a totally different outfit.

When I got home from church, I started the search for the shoe and was unsuccessful. I searched for it all afternoon, until it was time to go back to church services. When I got home that night, I called my niece, Asa. She reads mysteries. I told Asa about how I had purchased a pair of shoes, brought them home and now couldn't find one, even after searching every single room in my house. She suggested that there was nothing mysterious going on, and I should calm down. She was sure I'd find the shoe.

Of course by now my husband is getting really irritated with me about the shoe. In fact, he got so tired of me going on and on about the shoe until he said, "Don't say anything else to me about that shoe!" That night before I went to bed, all worn out and puzzled, I decided I would pray about the shoe. I had done everything else. I had looked everywhere. Only God knew the whereabouts of the shoe.

I sent up a bold prayer to God asking Him to lead me to my shoe. "Lord, you know where my shoe is. Please reveal its location." I prayed to God about my shoe like I prayed about anything else. I didn't think of my request as too small or petty. In fact, I wondered why I hadn't done it earlier.

The next morning, I woke up with the shoe on my mind. It had become somewhat of a burden, something I couldn't find a place of peace for. First of all, it made no sense that I couldn't find the shoe after searching the entire house. I had called my mom and she thought she was sure I tried the shoes on when we got home from shopping that night. I decided to call the shoe store where I bought the shoes to see if they had another pair I could purchase. They said they didn't have another pair in my size. Then, I decided to go to one of the stores down the street from where I live. I saw the shoe on their online store but in a different color. I thought, "Maybe I'll buy a different color, or maybe they'll have the silver shoe." No such luck. The store I went to had the shoe in brown but it was nothing near as cute as the silver one. I got back in my car frustrated and disgusted and drove away from the store. I kept driving. When I stopped, I was parked in the parking lot at the outlet mall where I purchased the shoes.

I wasn't sure what my plan of action was. I had already called the store where I purchased the shoes and was told they didn't have my size. I got out of my car and started walking. I went into a couple of shoe stores and asked if they had the shoes I was looking for. "No" was the answer. Then I saw the store where I purchased the shoes. "Oh well," I thought. "It's worth a try." I went into the store and walked over to the shoes. One of the silver shoes was on display. I already knew they didn't have my size, but the words just came out anyway. "Miss, do you have that silver shoe in a size nine?" She answered, "I'll check." She was gone a few minutes. When she came back, she said, "No I don't have that color in a nine, but I have a nine in the gold." I responded, "No, thanks." As much as I tried to get up from the little bench I was sitting on and walk out, I couldn't. It was as though something was holding me there. I stood up, but instead of walking out, I walked over to the silver shoe that was on display. I picked it up and admired it. In an instant, a thought came to mind. "Look at the size." I turned the shoe over and couldn't believe what I saw. I thought to myself, "Oh my goodness! It's a nine! Lord, yes!"

I calmed down just enough to ask the attendant, "Miss, can you please go see if you can find the mate to this shoe? It's a nine. I know you said you don't have this in a size nine, but there must be a mate." The lady left, but she didn't come right back. She was gone for several minutes. As I sat there holding the shoe and waiting for her, it all became so vividly clear. At that moment, I could have shouted right there in the store while the lady was gone to look for the shoe that I knew she was not going to find. I realized then, she would never find the mate because it was at my house.

When the lady came back from searching for the shoe, she was empty handed. I asked, "Miss, you couldn't find it could you?" "No," she responded. I said to her, "That's the mate to a shoe I have at home. I purchased a pair of shoes about two weeks ago, and I've been looking for the mate. When I opened my box, there was only one shoe. I thought I had misplaced it. But that's not the case. This is the mate to my shoe. The woman looked a little puzzled as she asked, "Do you have your receipt?" I said to her, "I'm going home to get my receipt and my shoe."

All the way home, I praised God. I thanked Him all the way home and all the way back to pick up my shoe and for the rest of the day. I thanked Him for answering my prayer. When I got back to the store, the lady had taken the shoe off the shelf, taped a note to it and placed it behind the counter. She knew it belonged to me, and she knew I would be back for it.

Nothing's Too Small for God

Nothing is too small or too petty to talk to God about. God can show up anywhere in any situation, big or small! One of the most encouraging and uplifting scriptures in the Bible is, *"Be anxious for nothing, but in everything by prayer and supplication, with thanksgiving, let your requests be made known to God"* (Philippians 4:6). I can't tell you how many times I've quoted this verse and encouraged myself in these words. If prayer is not a priority in your life, you're missing out on one of the greatest spiritual blessings you could ever experience. Prayer is one of the greatest tools a Christian can possess and one of the greatest gifts God has ever given.

You likely have a telephone. In fact, you may have a phone connected in your home attached to a phone jack called a landline. In addition, you likely have a mobile phone, one you carry with you. In fact, if you're like most people, you take your mobile or cell phone with you just about everywhere you go. It's amazing how we sometimes act as though we don't know what we'd do without our cell phones. You'd never know there was a time when we didn't have them. They are such a part of our everyday lives. We treat them like precious jewels. If you're like many, if you leave home and forget your cell phone, you will turn around and drive all the way back to get it. That's how important it is. It's the means by which you communicate with others, and if you don't have your cell phone with you at all times, you're afraid you might miss some important communications.

You use your phone for all kinds of communications. You use it to communicate with friends when you just need someone to talk to. You use it to communicate with the doctor's office when you need to make an appointment. You use it to communicate with your boss when you don't feel well and need to take the day off. You use it to communicate with your husband when you know you're going to be late coming home from work. You use it to communicate with your children when you don't know where they are. You use it to communicate with the person you're dating. You just want to hear their voice. You use it to communicate with the plumber when you need someone to fix the leak in the sink. You use it to communicate with the teacher when you want to know why your child received a low grade. Telephone communications are a very common part of life, and just like you commonly pick up the phone and communicate with other individuals, communicating with God should be just as common. Prayer is powerful. There are great Bible stories that demonstrate God's faithfulness and the fact that He answers prayers. Perhaps you're familiar with the story of Hezekiah.

A man named Hezekiah was sick, and God sent a prophet named Isaiah to tell Hezekiah to get his house in order because he was going to die. Hezekiah's response was prayer. The Bible says, *"Then Hezekiah turned his face toward the wall, and prayed to the Lord, and said, 'Remember now, O Lord, I pray, how I have walked before You in truth and with a loyal heart, and have done what is good in Your sight.' And Hezekiah wept bitterly"* (Isaiah 38:2-3). God heard Hezekiah's prayer, and He sent a message to him by the prophet Isaiah. He said, *"Go and tell Hezekiah, thus says the Lord, the God of David your father: 'I have heard your prayer, I have seen your tears; surely I will add to your days fifteen years'"* (Isaiah 38:5). God answers prayers.

How's your prayer life? How often do you go to God in prayer? If you were to calculate the number of times in a day you pick up your phone to communicate with others and compare it with the number of times you lift up your heart and pray to God, would there be a great difference in the numbers? I would venture to say, you likely communicate with others a lot more than you communicate with God.

Communicating with God is a privilege. It's also a gift, something He's given to every Christian. If you've ever experienced receiving a gift, the first thing you likely did was opened the gift. When you don't pray, you're simply ignoring or failing to open a precious gift. You're missing out on precious, valuable time in the presence of God.

Obstacles to Prayer

One of the greatest obstacles to prayer is a lack of time. The reason you may not spend enough time in prayer could very well be a lack of time. You simply don't have time. Perhaps when you get down on your knees to pray, before you know it, your head is slumped over and you're fast asleep. Does this describe you? When you crawl in bed with the intent of saying a prayer before you go to sleep, before you can even say, "Father in heaven," you're fast asleep. When you tell yourself the first thing you're going to do when you hit the floor in the morning is pray, before you know it, you're dressed and out the door, rushing to get to work with not enough time to pray. You just don't have time to pray. You just don't have time to pray.

Perhaps you're one of those persons who think you need twenty or thirty minutes to pray, and if you don't have such, you just don't pray. You think prayers have to be long and drawn out, something you have to set aside time for and plan for. That's not the case. Now, don't get me wrong. It's always a good idea to set aside prayer time, that special time you spend in the presence of God pouring out your heart to Him. But when time won't allow such, God accepts quick, short and to the point prayers. I know this is the case because the Bible says, "*Pray without ceasing*" (1 Thessalonians 5:17). Now if we are to literally pray without ceasing, that would mean we would spend twenty-four hours a day with our hearts lifted up in prayer. We would do nothing but pray. But that's not what the scripture means. Instead, it gives us permission to offer up periods of prayer that may be short, quick and to the point. For example, just the words, "Thank you Lord;" believe it or not, that's a prayer. "Lord, help me!" That's a prayer. "Lord, heal me." That's a prayer. These are nothing more than short and to the point prayers. And the great thing about praying lots of short prayers is, it keeps you in constant communication with the Lord all throughout the day, and before you know it, you'll find yourself communicating with God just as much as you communicate with all those people you talk to on your phone. Start praying right now. "Lord, thank you for getting me to work safely." "Lord, thank you for getting my children home safely." "Lord, thank you for my health." "Lord, give me the answer I need." Also, those things you might think of as being petty and small, pray those prayers too. Nothing's too small for God. "Lord, thank you for the green light." "Lord, thank you for the parking space." "Lord, thank you for helping me find my keys." "Lord, I'm so thankful there were no bills in the mail today!"

Get into the habit of having a prayer on your heart at all times. When you begin to practice this, it may actually motivate you to start setting aside prayer time with God. Constantly having a prayer on your heart could make you crave more time with the Lord. You may find yourself hungering and thirsting after time with Him. The Bible says, "*Draw near to God and He will draw near to you*" (James 4:8). If time management is an obstacle to your prayer life, short prayers may be just the answer for you.

Another obstacle to prayer for some women is thinking because your husband is the spiritual leader in your home, you don't have to pray. You feel you can just leave the praying to Him.

You are required to have your own relationship with God, and that relationship is separate and apart from the relationship your husband has with Him. You've got to "*work out your own salvation with fear and trembling*" (Philippians 2:12). "*So then each of us shall give account of himself to God*" (Romans 14:12). You cannot borrow your husband's prayer life. Just because your husband is praying, "Thank you Lord," doesn't mean you don't have to pray, "Thank you Lord." Just because your husband is praying, "Lord, bless our children," doesn't mean you don't have to pray for your children. Just because your husband is praying, "Lord, heal my wife's disease," doesn't mean you don't have to pray for yourself. Just like your husband needs his own prayer life and his own line of communication with the Lord, you need your own. Now that doesn't mean God doesn't answer the prayers your husband prays on your behalf, because he will. Your husband can pray for you and his prayers can be answered. But that doesn't take away your prayer responsibilities. Look at it this way. If Jesus had to have His own line of communication with God, why on earth would you think you don't need to have your own? Of all people, even Jesus prayed.

"Then Jesus came with them to a place called Gethsemane, and said to the disciples, „Sit here while I go and pray over there'" (Matthew 26:36). *"Now in the morning, having risen a long while before daylight, He went out and departed to a solitary place; and there He prayed"* (Mark 1:35). *"So He Himself often withdrew into the wilderness and prayed"* (Luke 5:16). *"Now it came to pass in those days that He went out to the mountain to pray, and continued all night in prayer to God"* (Luke 6:12). If Jesus prayed, then praying is certainly something that's required of you, and no one can do it for you.

There's another obstacle to prayer worth mentioning. You may be one who believes God doesn't accept your prayers unless you're down on your knees, and if you're not in a place where you can actually get into that particular posture, you don't pray. If that's the position you take, just think of how much you are limiting yourself when it comes to praying. Unless you're at home every day or have total control of your time, you're not likely going to find many opportunities to actually get down on your knees and pray during the course of a day. So when you believe this is the posture you have to be in for God to hear your prayers, you limit the amount of time you spend in prayer. On the other hand, if you have opportunities to get down on your knees and pray, by all means do so. There is certainly a message in this posture. It's a posture that expresses an humble attitude or spirit. It expresses reverence and respect. However, it's not a requirement for God to accept your prayers. God is more concerned with the posture of your heart than the posture of your body.

Pray For Others

Another important aspect of prayer is praying for others. *"Let each of you look out not only for his own interests, but also for the interests of others"* (Philippians 2:4). *"Confess your trespasses to one another, and pray for one another, that you may be healed. The effective, fervent prayer of a righteous man avails much*" (James 5:16). It's a blessing when you've got righteous people in your life who can pray for you, and it's even more of a blessing when you are the righteous person and can go to God on behalf of others. When was the last time you prayed for someone? Do you make it a point to pray for others, or do you only say prayers that would benefit you?

Perhaps you've had someone say to you, "Pray for me." That's pretty common in my circle of friends, family members and church family. There was a time when I'd totally forget a person had requested that I pray for them. By the time I said a prayer, I had totally forgotten. I started to realize, if someone requested that I pray for them and I agreed, it wasn't good to forget to do it. To keep this from continuously happening, I started praying for the person as soon as they made the request. Now when someone calls and wants me to pray for them, I pray immediately. In fact, I will usually pray right there on the spot. If I meet a friend in passing and they say, "Pray for me," as soon as they've passed by, I start praying. This has helped me fulfill my prayer requests.

Sending up a prayer on behalf of someone else is one of the greatest gifts you can give a person. Did you know there are persons who are no longer sick and in the hospital because somebody prayed for them? Did you know someone found a job because somebody prayed for them? Did you know there's someone out there who received a financial blessing because somebody prayed for them? Did you know there's a young person out there who didn't get what he or she deserved because somebody prayed for them? Someone out there made it through a storm because somebody prayed for them. Some person out there never went through a storm because somebody prayed for them. There's always somebody you can pray for. If you don't have anyone to pray for, pray for me!

You're likely familiar with the story of Job in the Old Testament. The Bible says Job "*was blameless and upright, and one who feared*

God and shunned evil" (Job 1:1). God allowed adversity to come upon Job. He allowed Satan to take and destroy everything Job owned. While Job was going through his challenges, three friends came to visit and console him. When they heard all that had happened to Job, they believed he had sinned and angered God to cause this calamity. However, this was not the case. Job's calamity was not due to sin. The Bible says Job prayed for his friends and when he did, the Lord restored his losses. *"And the Lord restored Job's losses when he prayed for his friends. Indeed the Lord gave Job twice as much as he had before"* (Job 42:10).

God smiles when you pray for others. There's a blessing in it. I believe the same blessings you request for others, God will give you those same blessings.

If you're not enjoying the privilege and blessing of prayer, you're missing out. You may be the person who doesn't pray because you're discouraged. You prayed for something you greatly desired, but God didn't answer. Perhaps a loved one was ill. You prayed but God took your loved one anyway. Or, perhaps your child has gone astray, and your prayers for his or her deliverance have gone unanswered. Maybe you prayed that you wouldn't be the one to get a pink slip on the job, but was laid off anyway. Maybe you prayed that somehow you'd have the money to pay the bills that were due, but your prayers went unanswered.

For the Christian who's striving to live a life of holiness, those who pray to God with a sincere heart, I don't believe there is any such thing as an unanswered prayer. God may not give you what you ask for, but He's always going to give you what you need, what's best for you. God has a larger view of life than you. You can't see any farther than what your eyes show you. But God can see the big picture, and He orchestrates your life and orders your steps according to the big picture. You won't always understand what He's doing. That's not possible. The Bible teaches, *"For my thoughts are not your thoughts, nor are your ways my ways, says the Lord. For as the heavens are higher than the earth, so are my ways higher than your ways, and my thoughts than your thoughts*" (Isaiah 55:8-9). While you will never understand everything God is doing in your life, you can rest assured; He has your best interest at heart.

Some of the things we ask for when we go to God in prayer, we don't realize what we're asking for. Sometimes when God doesn't give us what we ask for, it actually could be a blessing in disguise. God already knows the outcome and consequences, and He grants us what we need according to His will and purpose. I'm glad I serve a God who knows what's best for me. I'm glad I serve a God who can see farther down the road than I can see; a God who can see what my life looks like five years from now, ten years from now, fifteen years from now, and His plans for me are according to where He wants me to be, not just today, but also in the future. We live in a world where we're used to instant gratification. We want things now. When we pray and ask God for something and we don't get it instantly, we lose faith, and in many cases, give up on God.

Trust God and believe He knows what's best for you. You should know beyond a doubt that *"all things work together for good to those who love God, to those who are the called according to His purpose"* (Romans 8:28). God knows you and He knows your every need.

The Right Connection

In today's time, communicating by phone isn't the only means of communicating. It's also common to communicate through social networking sites where you build a network of friends. There are those who have built networks of thousands of friends and can interact with them on a daily basis. If you've created networks on sites such as Facebook, keep in mind the positives as well as the negatives. Social networking sites are great for keeping in touch with friends as well as networking for business purposes. However, if you're not careful, you could find yourself spending an enormous amount of time on a social networking site, time you could be spending in prayer. When you spend an enormous amount of time on these sites, you're robbing God of time that should be committed to Him. Also, be careful of whom you connect with. Not all connections are godly connections. And while you can make worthwhile connections on social networking sites that can be a benefit to you in your personal as well as professional life, the most important connection you can make is a connection with the Lord.

When you connect with the Lord, He requires something of you. *"I beseech you therefore, brethren, by the mercies of God, that you present your bodies a living sacrifice, holy, acceptable to God, which is your reasonable service. And do not be conformed to this world, but be transformed by the renewing of your mind, that you may prove what is that good and acceptable and perfect will of God"* (Romans 12:1-2). When you add Jesus as a friend, it may be necessary to let go of some of your other friends. You can't be a friend of Jesus and also be a friend of the world. *"Do you not know that friendship with the world is enmity with God? Whoever therefore wants to be a friend of the world makes himself an enemy of God"* (James 4:4). Have fellowship and friendship with the Lord through prayer. In all of life, He is the best connection you can make and the best friend you can have.

FOR DISCUSSION

1. We can see examples throughout the Bible of men and women who prayed to God and God answered their prayers. Find, discuss and share Scriptures to support other examples. Start with King Hezekiah in 2 Kings 20.

2. What are some things that hinder us from building a stronger, more consistent prayer life?

3. I Thessalonians 5:17 says, "Pray without ceasing." What does this mean?

4. Examine Philippians 4:6. This Scripture is a reference to the term, "Let go and let God." It's our nature to give it to God, only to find ourselves taking it back. As women, what are some reasons we oftentimes struggle with letting go? Share a time when you struggled with letting go.

5. What are some emotions and circumstances we invite into our lives when we cannot "let go and let God?"

6. In 2 Kings 20:2-3, King Hezekiah prayed to God. As he prayed, he reminded God of some things. What did he remind God of? What messages do we get from this?

7. Sometimes our prayer life suffers because we feel we don't have time to pray. While God is not concerned with the length of our prayers, what are some things He is more concerned with? See Philippians 4:6, 1 John, 5:14 and Mark 11:24.

8. One of the greatest aspects of prayer is the fact that we can use it to petition God on behalf of others. What does the Bible teach about praying for others? Give Scriptures, starting with Ephesians 6:18.

9. Perhaps you have known someone who wasn't able to pray because they were angry with God. Even though they prayed for a favorable outcome, an unfortunate circumstance happened anyway. They blame God for not preventing it. If you have ever had such experience, share it. What advice

would you give to someone who is struggling with anger towards God? What Scriptures would you use? Start with Romans 8:35-39.

10. Do you have a Facebook account? If so, how many friends do you have? Should Jesus be one of your friends? Would he approve of the nature of your Facebook posts? Give examples of good, Christian Facebook etiquette.

Chapter 3

Recognize It's Not All About You

"My New Sweater"

*"Let nothing be done through selfish ambition or conceit,
but in lowliness of mind let each esteem others
better than himself" (Philippians 2:3).*

Being in a family of seven children didn't leave much room for feeling special, garnering attention and feeling like, "It's all about me!" However, I can remember an occasion when I was made to feel like I was the only child.

I couldn't have been more than five years old. I would work out in the old shed with my dad. We'd fill huge sacks with feed for farm animals. I would hold the sacks while my dad poured in the feed. One day, my dad and I were working pretty late. He had worked much harder than I had, shoveling feed and dumping it into the sacks. In fact, drops of sweat filled his face.

What happened that evening surprised me. My dad picked up a huge pile of feed and dumped it into the sack. Then, he put down his shovel, reached into his back pocket, pulled out his wallet and handed me one dollar. I was not expecting it and was totally taken by surprise.

When we finished our work, I ran to the house to show my mom and my siblings what Dad had given me. Of course my mother convinced me that it would be a good idea if she took my pay and placed it in a safe place. She said, "I'm going to put this away. We'll go shopping and buy you a new sweater."

My mom kept her word. Later that week, we drove into town. We went into the department store and bought me a brand new white sweater that I absolutely loved. In fact, not long afterwards, my mom took my little sister and me to a photographer and we took pictures. I had on my new white sweater.

The memory of being rewarded by my dad and then taken to the store to purchase a new sweater is one of my fondest childhood memories. It was one of those occasions when I was made to feel that I was valued.

Selfish Behaviors

It's our nature to want to be valued, but the problems come when our desire to be valued turns into selfish behavior, and we develop an attitude that says, "It's all about me." When I was growing up, my siblings and I really didn't know what it meant to have a selfish attitude. We expected to share. We came into the world sharing everything from our bedroom to our clothes.

When you're selfish, your main focus is yourself. You have the "It's all about me" attitude. Instead of making sacrifices for others, you sacrifice others for your own good. Does this describe you? Do you have the "It's all about me" attitude? "*For I say, through the grace given to me, to everyone who is among you, not to think of himself more highly than he ought to think, but to think soberly, as God has dealt to each one a measure of faith*" (Romans 12:3). "*For if anyone thinks himself to be something, when he is nothing, he deceives himself*" (Galatians 6:3).

Suppose you have a good friend and every time the two of you go out to dinner, it always has to be his favorite restaurant. He never wants to eat at the restaurants you suggest. Whenever you go to the movies, it has to be a movie of his choice. You never get to pick the movie, and when you make suggestions for movie titles, he refuses to see the one you want to see. Or, suppose you need a helping hand from a neighbor, but it seems like she's never available. Last weekend when you needed to drop off your car at the dealership for an early morning service check, you asked if she would mind getting up and following you so you would have a ride home. She said, "No, I'm sleeping in." Although she never seems to be able to accommodate your needs, you are always there for her. In fact, just recently, you've done a couple of favors for her. You dropped off her daughter at school one morning so your neighbor could get to work early to prepare for a meeting. You picked up her daughter from school one afternoon so she could work late. If a person in your life consistently shows this type of selfish attitude, this relationship can easily turn unhealthy.

Perhaps you're the person who has been accused of possessing an attitude of selfishness. If so, examine your behavior. Don't just dismiss this idea and think you're being wrongly criticized. Take the accusations seriously and examine the claim. Also, recognize that selfishness doesn't just show itself in only one of your relationships. If you've been accused of displaying a selfish attitude with your friends, chances are, you show this same attitude with family members and others. Do some investigating and find out if you really are a selfish person. Ask people you're close to, those who will be honest. Co-workers can tell if you exhibit selfish behavior. They likely spend more waking hours with you than anyone else. Ask a sibling, even your parents if they see you as a selfish individual. And when they tell you the truth and confirm your selfish behavior, be able to accept their criticism. This can be healthy and can motivate you to make changes. I can think back and remember times when my mother accused me of selfish behavior. I hated it when she would say to me, "You're just selfish!" I didn't like this label, so I started examining myself and tried to see myself from her perspective. And yes, I did make changes, and those changes were for the better.

Where Selfishness Comes From

Where does selfish behavior come from? Perhaps you were raised in an environment where you lived a very comfortable lifestyle never being afforded opportunities to learn the value of looking out for the interests of others. Instead, you grew up surrounded by individuals whose focus was more on making sure you had the things you wanted. Their focus was on making sure you weren't lacking in any of your wants. Learning to look out for the interests of others sometimes requires sacrifice, so if you never learned the value of this, you likely never learned to sacrifice.

To sacrifice means to give up something you value so someone else can have something. But instead of you making sacrifices, someone made sacrifices for you and unfortunately, they never gave you the opportunity to do the same. When you grow up lacking in experiences that teach you how and why you should look out for the interests of others, you will likely grow into adulthood with a selfish attitude.

Does this describe you? If so and you're a parent, you could be teaching your children these same negative behaviors and attitudes. Are you guilty of instilling this type of behavior in your children? Many children today have more material goods than we ever thought of having when we were growing up. The bedrooms of many children today are fully equipped with all of the latest technology: telephone, cable or satellite TV, computer and all kinds of other electronic gadgets. Does this sound like your child? Perhaps your child's closet is full of all of the name brand labels. All they have to do is ask for what they want and you buy it. They see the neighbor's kids with something they want and you get it for them. They come home and tell you about something someone at school has, you get it for them. You could very well be raising a child to have the attitude that says, "It's all about me, me, and me!"

Realize that you are doing more harm than good when you raise your children in a way that teaches them the "It's all about me" attitude. When you don't teach children the value of looking out for the interests of others, you are taking away one of those foundational principles from their lives that is necessary for a successful adult life. You are raising children who do not know how to properly love others. When they grow up and get out in the workforce, they may have difficulty being a team player. Due to their self-centered nature, they may be unable to function properly in a setting where it's necessary to share ideas and work for the good of the entire team. When they grow up and get married, they are ill equipped to function in a marriage relationship because they have not been taught how to look out for the interests of others.

Also, as you raise your children to learn selfish behavior, you are teaching them to be ungrateful and unthankful. Begin to observe them. You may see an attitude of being unappreciative of the sacrifices you make to give them what they want. As you observe them, perhaps you will see an attitude in them that says, "It's your duty to give me what I want. It's what you're supposed to do."

When you teach your children to work for and earn what they get, then they will learn to appreciate it. Instead of giving them what they want, give them the opportunity to earn it. Give them chores to do around the house that will allow them to earn cash to purchase what they want. This gives them the opportunity to learn money management skills. Or, perhaps you give them an allowance. If so, teach them to save when they want some special purchase. When you do this, you are teaching your children how to appreciate the things they acquire. When they have to spend their own money on something, they will appreciate it a lot more.

Another way to instill an attitude of selflessness and a thankful heart in children is take them with you when you go out to perform acts of charity or visit someone who is ill. Your child needs to see you performing acts of love, acts of charity. Allow them to become involved, serve and help others so they can develop a compassionate spirit. Explain to them what you are doing and why. When you go out and visit someone who is ill, if there are no health risks for either the child or the patient, take your child with you and allow them to experience this teaching or training opportunity. Let me share with you something I once experienced.

I didn't really know the person who passed away. I went to the funeral to support my sister-in-law. The deceased was her aunt. At any rate, a young woman stood up at the funeral and went over to the microphone to share some words about the deceased. The words she spoke were so appropriate for the subject of instilling an attitude of selflessness and empathy in our children.

The young woman introduced herself as the niece of the deceased. She went on to talk about how when she was just a child, she would often go with her aunt to visit a lady who was sick. She said her aunt would cook food and they would take it to the lady. When they got there, the young woman said she would watch her aunt prepare the food, and then she would even feed the lady because she couldn't feed herself. Her aunt would do this even when the lady had other relatives there who could have done this for her. And that's the part that was so puzzling for the little girl as she watched her aunt perform this act.

The young woman said that one day she decided to ask her aunt about this. She asked, "Why do you take food to that lady and feed her when she has relatives there who could do this?" According to the woman, her aunt answered, "Honey, it doesn't matter that others are there. You just remember this. There are some things God wants you to do. It doesn't matter what others are doing. When God gives you something to do, you do it."

The young woman spoke of how those words that were planted in her when she was just a child have stayed with her through the years and how her experience of going to visit this sick person with her aunt instilled in her the importance of loving others and sharing in the lives of others with your time and efforts.

Your children need to see you engaging in these kinds of acts as you teach them to do the same. You may not be able to see how this is making a difference in their young lives now, but if you are consistent in making sure they are exposed to these kinds of acts, the effects of this are sure to show up in their lives somewhere down the line.

Selfishness in Marriage

Your marriage relationship may be just the place your selfish behavior reveals itself. You may find yourself putting unrealistic demands on your spouse simply because you want what you want. You put your needs before his. You want your spouse to do this or do that. But when you're asked to do something, you don't have time. You're too busy. You don't feel like it. That's selfish behavior.

I can remember an experience in my marriage that taught me the value of husband and wife looking out for each other.

It was Saturday night just before bedtime. I was exhausted and couldn't wait to go to bed. Before I went upstairs, I looked for my cell phone. Each night before I go to bed, I place it on the table next to the bed. "Where in the world did I put my phone?" I kept asking myself this question. In my exhaustion, I finally gave up looking for the phone and made my way up the stairs to bed. My husband, Quincy, was already fast asleep, and had been for quite some time.

I rolled out of bed around seven-thirty in the morning. Quincy had already left for work. As I made my way toward the bathroom, something caught my eye. Right next to the sink was my cell phone. I knew I didn't leave it there, and I knew it wasn't there when I went to bed. As I stood there and stared at the phone, a wave of emotion hit me and I almost dropped a tear. I thought about how I had spent so much time the night before searching for my phone. My mind turned to my husband. I immediately knew what happened. During his early morning routine, which includes getting up, watching the news, and getting dressed for work, he found my cell phone.

I thought to myself, "Why did my husband take the time to bring my phone upstairs and place it where I could see it? Why didn't he just leave it where it was?" I already knew the answer. When he found my phone, he immediately knew it was in an unusual place. He knew I had lost it. I'm sure he thought to himself, "She probably looked for this phone all night long."

I stood there and tried to focus on my husband's small, thoughtful, yet loving actions. But instead, in those few moments, all of my shortcomings as a wife were brought to the surface. I stood there feeling like a light was shining brightly on my faults and failures. I thought about this small act of love my husband had shown, and then I thought about how many times I have simply forgotten to do some small thing he asked me to do, and how he never complains about my inadequacies. I thought about what the Bible says about real love. *"Love suffers long and is kind; love does not envy; love does not parade itself, is not puffed up; does not behave rudely, does not seek its own, is not provoked, thinks no evil"* (1 Corinthians 13:4-5). I thought of the many times I have fallen short in demonstrating love to my husband in the little things of life.

I later shared with my husband how his kind, loving act made me feel so special, and I apologized for my shortcomings. I realized that if couples are not careful, selfishness can creep into a marriage unnoticed. It's like the frog in hot water. Because the temperature was turned up little by little, he didn't notice the water heating up. Before he knew it, he was sitting in boiling water.

If your status is married and you plan to remain married, don't be selfish. Don't possess an attitude that says, "It's all about me." "It's my way or no way." "If you don't like it, that's too bad." "You can't have that because I need this."

If you're single and set in your ways, stay single. Even if you think you've met Mr. Right, don't say, "I do." Perhaps you're used to managing your own household, having nobody to answer to, spending all of your money on what you choose to spend it on. You're not used to having to answer to someone else; not used to having to let someone know where you're going and what you're doing. Well, if you're not going to change, the best advice I can give you is, remain single. If you try to transfer these same actions, behaviors and attitudes into a marriage relationship, you'll likely later regret your decision. The actions that demonstrate the "It's all about me" attitude can quickly become selfishness in a relationship, and you can easily find your relationship becoming toxic and unhealthy.

One of the greatest dangers of selfish behavior is the fact that it's difficult to detect in self. If you're a selfish person, you likely have a hard time admitting you have the attitude that says, "It's all about me." You've likely convinced yourself that what you do is necessary, and there's nothing wrong with your behavior. You've convinced yourself that you're not the problem. Others have the problem. You feel a sense of superiority. You feel you are always right. Perhaps you've heard the saying, *"You can't fix the problem until you admit there is a problem."* Well, the same can be said of a person with a selfish attitude. You can't rid yourself of a selfish attitude until you're willing to admit you have an attitude that says, "It's all about me."

Overcoming Selfish Behaviors

God's way of overcoming selfishness is by replacing it with love. If you've ever heard of the great entertainer, Tina Turner, you've likely heard the song she sang entitled, "What's Love Got to Do With It?" Love has everything to do with it. *"And though I have the gift*

39

of prophecy, and understand all mysteries and all knowledge, and though I have all faith, so that I could remove mountains, but have not love, I am nothing" (1 Corinthians 13:2).

It would be nice to have the gift of prophecy and be able to understand all mysteries, and it would certainly be nice to have mountain-moving faith. But even if you were somehow able to possess all of these, the Bible teaches, it would mean absolutely nothing if you don't know how to love.

The world as a whole, even including the church, would be a much better place if we would exercise the command to *"love your neighbor as yourself"* (Matthew 22:39). If everybody everywhere would exercise this command, all wars going on in the world would cease. Wouldn't it be a healing, sobering sight to see soldiers throwing down their weapons and embracing the enemy with a hug? Can you imagine that? The wars fought right here in our own country would come to an end. The war on drugs, race wars, cultural wars, political wars, religious wars all would come to an end if all of mankind would exercise the command to love. The wars going on in the home would come to an end; the struggle between husband and wife to stay together, the battle with the world for our children, and the struggle for positions and power in society.

These are just a few of the wars, conflicts, and battles going on today, and there's only one thing that can bring them to a peaceful end and guarantee that the days ahead are filled with peace. Love can bring peace where there's turmoil; an unconditional, sacrificial love where every person takes him or herself out of the way and works for the good of others, recognizing, "It's not all about me!"

God is the author of love. *"For God so loved the world that He gave His only begotten Son, that whoever believes in Him should not perish but have everlasting life"* (John 3:16). God demonstrated the kind of love He wants us to have. However, even as Christians, on so many fronts we're missing the point of what God is looking for in us. We think we've got God all figured out. There's a story in the

Bible; Luke 10:25-37, of a man who was beaten half dead and left by the side of the road. The person who stopped to render aid was the most unlikely person to stop. The two men whom we would think certainly would have stopped to render aid did not, and they were known as upright men of God, a priest and a Levite.

Perhaps you are doing what one might call many wonderful works. But the question is, does love have anything to do with what you are doing? Perhaps you attend church services regularly. You're in church every time the doors open; Sunday morning, Sunday evening, and if there's something going on at the church during the weekdays, you're there also. You put forth a huge effort to look like a Christian, to look like your life is dedicated to the Lord. You visit the sick and give to those in need. However, if what you're doing is not done in love, you are nothing more than a clanging cymbal as Paul puts it. *"Though I speak with the tongues of men and of angels, but have not love, I have become sounding brass or a clanging cymbal"* (1 Corinthians 13:1).

A selfish attitude, or an attitude that says, "It's all about me," can be erased with love. God is looking into your heart. He's judging you on how much you love not only Him, but how much you love your neighbor, how much you look out for the interests of others out of a genuine, loving heart, not out of a grudging spirit of necessity. "What's love got to do with it?" Love has everything to do with it.

Having a sacrificial, selfless spirit is God's will for your life. *"Let nothing be done through selfish ambition or conceit, but in lowliness of mind let each esteem others better than himself. Let each of you look out not only for his own interests, but also for the interests of others"* (Philippians 2:3-4). Learn what God expects from you. *"If my people who are called by My name will humble themselves, and pray and seek My face, and turn from their wicked ways, then I will hear from heaven, and will forgive their sin and heal their land"* (2 Chronicles 7:14). The Lord is always willing and waiting for you to turn from evil to good, waiting for you to seek His face. He wants you to humble yourself, take the focus off yourself and focus on Him.

Being selfless is not to be mistaken with possessing a spirit of weakness, nor does it mean possessing a spirit where you don't speak up for yourself, and you allow others to take advantage of you and push you around. That's not what it means to have a selfless spirit. You can look out for the interests of others, have a yielding, submissive spirit, stand down and let someone go before you; you can do all of these and still be a person of strength, a person of character, someone who stands up for yourself, someone who recognizes that your needs are also important. The key is to use wisdom. Learn to choose your battles wisely. Recognize that in matters of opinion, it's all right to let someone else have their way. Know when to take a stand. Not everything is worth fighting for. Let God's Word guide your actions and behavior. Healthy relationships produce love. Selfish relationships produce division and strife. Get rid of that attitude that says, "It's all about me." It's not all about you!

FOR DISCUSSION

1. Read and examine Romans 12:3. What can be some of the consequences of thinking of yourself more highly than you ought to think?

2. Give suggestions for how to balance caring for your own physical, emotional and spiritual wellbeing, with helping, serving and being a caretaker for others?

3. As women, our lives can become pretty hectic and busy. We can find ourselves wearing many hats; always being asked to do something for someone. Some women feel guilty when they say "no." When is it ok to say "no?" Does saying "no" mean you are selfish? When does saying "no" become selfishness?

4. From where can selfishness get its roots?

5. In relationships, what are some of the consequences of selfish behaviors?

6. What does sacrifice have to do with looking out for the interests of others? Discuss and relate Genesis 13.

7. On page 41, the author shares a story about a woman who took care of someone who had relatives who could have taken on this responsibility. When the woman was questioned by her niece about this, how did she respond? Why was this an appropriate response?

8. What are some valuable lessons we can learn from the woman who cared for the sick. What can we learn from her niece?

9. When a person who has been single most of their life decides to get married; considering the phrase, "Old habits are hard to break," what are some challenges they might face in a marriage?

10. What should a spirit of selfishness be replaced with? Read Luke 10:30-37. Discuss lessons we can take from the man who stopped to render assistance. What was significant about the fact that the other two didn't stop to help?

Chapter 4

Learn To Forgive

"The Murder—Suicide"

"But if you do not forgive,
neither will your Father in heaven
forgive your trespasses" (Mark 11:26).

It was a normal fall morning. I got up, got dressed and went to work at the advertising agency where I had worked for about three years. The department I worked in at the time was new to me, but I was getting used to it. As usual, around noon, I grabbed my purse and headed out the door for lunch. On nice, sunny days, my lunch hour might consist of a salad and a trip to a nearby park where I would watch joggers and runners make their way around the track. However, on this particular day, I had a few errands to run. I finished my work and headed out the door to the parking garage.

After running my errands, I headed back to the office. When I got there, as I was walking down the hallway to my cubicle, I heard a voice from behind calling my name. I turned around to see who it was, and noticed that it was the director of Human Resources. I stopped to greet her. She handed me a piece of pink paper with a name and phone number on it and said, "It's a message for you." I looked at the paper and it was the name and phone number of a close, personal friend of mine. I wasn't sure why she would have taken a call from him. I didn't ask any questions. I went to my cubicle, sat down at my desk and dialed his number.

It was the longest drive to East Texas I had ever taken. After I talked to my friend, everything seemed to go in slow motion. I vaguely remember leaving the office and going to pick up my ten-year old son from school. We drove the two-hour drive to my mother's house in silence. In fact, silence was the only thing I remember about the two-hour trip home. My mind was cloudy and I felt disconnected from my body.

When we arrived at my mother's house, there were already people gathered there. I greeted my mother and asked, "Mama, is it true? What happened?" She responded, "Yes. It's true." The ball in my stomach seemed to get larger. I felt like I was going to stop breathing at any moment. I asked again, "What happened?" My mother went on to explain that she had gotten the call from the police department that morning around nine o'clock and was told to come. They told her there had been a shooting and her daughter was the victim. My older sister had been shot and killed.

As information began to unfold, I found out that my sister, who was a widow with two small children, had been dating someone and was planning to end the relationship. She had actually gone to work that morning, but because she was anxious and in a hurry to end the relationship, she left work and went to the home of the man she was dating, not knowing that's where her life would end.

Trying to digest what was happening was challenging to say the least. Trying to understand how someone could commit such a horrible act was not possible. It was difficult to understand how anyone could have the audacity to make such a decision, the decision to take my sister's life and remove her from the lives of her two young children and from her family and friends.

My mental and emotional states were so mixed up and confused until the tears wouldn't even come. Then as I learned the details of my sister's death, it was even more upsetting and disturbing. The man shot her outside his house, left her on the ground to die, went inside his house and shot himself in the head. He, too, was dead.

A couple of days passed before we were able to go view our loved one's remains. But I wasn't as anxious to visit my sister's remains, as I was to view the remains of her murderer. As I drove up to the funeral home where his body had been prepared for viewing, I saw a few people standing outside. I remember walking slowly up the aisle. As I got closer to the casket, I could see his face. I stood there staring at him and silently crying out in my spirit, begging God to torment his soul.

Anger and Grief

This life-changing experience happened many years ago. However, I still remember the emotional pain I felt and the anger and grief that consumed me.

The combination of anger and grief had the potential of being spiritually and even physically damaging. However, it was difficult for me to think in terms of the spiritual and physical effects of my emotions. In fact, it seemed as though my spiritual mind had left me. In the days and months that followed, I had to find a way to cope with my emotions of anger and bitterness as I grieved the loss of my older sister.

Losing a loved one is never easy. But when you think of losing someone to death, you normally think of it in the context of old age, or perhaps some type of illness, and not in the context of a murder—suicide, or some other gruesome act. The difficulty in managing my emotional and mental states was in the thought that my sister died unnecessarily. She didn't die because of old age or an illness. My grieving was exacerbated by the fact that she died unnecessarily at the hands of a person who simply made a decision to take her life because he wanted to. Her death was a decision made by another person who didn't have the right to make the decision. It was unfair and unnecessary for her to die.

I cried a lot of tears in the days following my sister's death. I had heard of what's called the grieving process, which is a set of stages you go through when you lose a loved one. Denial is the first step, while acceptance is supposed to be the final step. Anger is somewhere in between the two, among other things like guilt and depression. The only thing that made my grief more bearable and made my mental and emotional states calm down was time. As the days and months went by, the loss became easier to bear and the tears came less frequently.

Forgiveness, the Best Medicine

Just as I experienced the loss of my sister and wanted to seek revenge, surely you've experienced situations where you've wanted to seek revenge against someone. The emotional pain that comes when you are deeply hurt can be even more painful than injuries that are inflicted on your physical body. When the pain is from a physical wound, when you trip and fall and hurt your knee, or jog around the track and pull a muscle, you can take medication for the wound, or put on an ice pack. You can find all kinds of medical remedies for a physical wound. And if you give it the proper attention, your wound will heal in no time.

It would be great if we could heal our wounded hearts the same way we heal a wounded leg, ankle, foot or toe. When someone hurts you, wouldn't it be nice to be able to rub on a little ointment to make the hurt go away? Unfortunately, it's not that simple. Forgiveness is the best medicine for a wounded heart, and forgiveness isn't always easy.

When you don't forgive, when you harbor resentment, you open yourself up to emotional and even physical illnesses. Anger and resentment can become like a cancer that starts out small but grows. It becomes metastasized just like cancer in the physical body. And before you know it, anger, bitterness and resentment have consumed you and are controlling you. When you don't forgive, you are basically allowing someone to control you. You make decisions based on what that person does. You calculate your actions based on that person. For example, you decide not to eat lunch in the break-room at work because you don't want to eat in the same room with someone who hurt you. If I had not learned to forgive the man who killed my sister, I would have been allowing a dead man to control me.

It's a lot easier to forgive when you have the Spirit of God in you. There are some things in life that are just too difficult for us to do alone. There's an Old Testament story of a man named Joseph. His brothers hated him to the point they put him in a pit, then sold him into slavery. If anyone had a reason to be bitter and vengeful, it surely was Joseph. But Joseph remained close to God. The Bible says, "*The Lord was with Joseph*" (Genesis 39:2). When you have been deeply hurt, it's easier to work through it when the Lord is with you.

Humility is an important element in the process of forgiving. You will never develop a heart of forgiveness if you are not willing to humble yourself. Your spirit should be one of lowliness and humility, and this spirit is inspired by love, even for the person who hurt you. I can remember in the days following the death of my sister, the family of the man who killed her came to our house to visit. This seemed awkward to me, but my mother greeted them with hugs. She showed humility and love toward them.

Pride is the opposite of humility and is one of our greatest obstacles to developing a heart of forgiveness. Pride will never allow you to humble yourself. Being humble helped my mother see the family of my sister's killer in a different perspective. She saw each of them as someone who deserved our sympathy and our love, someone made in God's image, and someone who needs God's grace and mercy. You too must see the person who harmed you through different lenses, from a different perspective. Then the forgiveness and healing can begin. When Joseph met his brothers again at a different time and different place, if he had looked at them as being evildoers, he could not have forgiven them. Instead, he looked at them through the eyes of love. He humbled himself and showed love to his family, in spite of what they had done to him.

To forgive someone is more for you than it is for the person who harmed you. That's a lesson I learned. The man I forgave couldn't hear me apologize for the hatred I felt. He couldn't feel a sense of relief when I forgave him. He was dead. But forgiving him did me a world of good. I could go on with my life and not be consumed with what he did. I no longer had to worry about him in his death having control over me.

When you learn to forgive, you recognize that God controls your life, and even though you don't understand everything that happens to you, you know that *"all things work together for good to those who love God, to those who are the called according to His purpose"* (Romans 8:28). When God's Holy Spirit lives in you, everything that happens to you is for your good. There's a lesson, a learning there for you, something to help you become the person God created you to be.

It's been more than twenty years since my sister was murdered. The house she and her children lived in is still standing. After her death, my brother and his family moved in and have since lived there and taken care of the property. Not long ago, an unfortunate incident took place on the property.

It was late evening, around eight o'clock. My brother was inside the house, probably playing his guitar, when he heard a loud noise. He walked outside to see what caused the noise, and he saw something lying in the front yard. Because of the late hour, he couldn't see clearly. As he walked closer, he could see that it was the body of a young man. Startled and shaken, my brother kneeled down and put his face close to the man to see if he was breathing. He heard him take a couple of breaths, and then the man died. He died right there in the front yard of the house my sister lived in before she was murdered. I later would learn that the deceased was the son of the man who killed my sister.

The man had a terrible automobile accident, and according to the local newspaper, "The man, who was not wearing a seatbelt at the time of the crash, was thrown from the vehicle." He lost control of his vehicle a short distance before the house and was thrown from the vehicle into the yard.

Needless to say this event brought back painful memories and reminded me of the lessons I learned years ago in forgiveness and humility. And since the loss of my sister, I've been faced with many other challenges in forgiveness. But I thank God that by the power of His Holy Spirit, He gives me strength to work through my challenges.

FOR DISCUSSION

1. Recall a time when your life was touched by physical violence such as a murder, losing a loved one in an auto accident, unexpected death from an illness, or some other circumstance that took the life of a loved one unexpectedly. While neither is easy to bear, discuss the depth of emotions that come with an unexpected circumstance compared to something you are more prepared for, such as losing a loved one to a long-term illness.

2. What is the one thing the Bible teaches that's common to all mankind when it comes to our appointment with death? Give the Scripture.

3. Joseph, the son of Jacob, in Genesis 37:3-4, was hated by his brothers, so they sold him into slavery. We see in Genesis 39:1-6 that Joseph experienced successes. What can his successes be attributed to? Did Joseph seek revenge against His brothers? Describe the meeting where Joseph revealed himself to his brothers in Genesis 45. What emotions do you think were strongest in the brothers of Joseph when they found out he was the brother they sold into slavery?

4. It takes a person with certain character traits to endure what Joseph endured. From all that we can read about Joseph, what would you say were some of his strongest character traits?

5. Describe the spiritual process the Bible teaches us to follow when we have been hurt or offended by a brother or sister. Give a supporting Scripture.

6. Domestic violence is an issue that is no stranger to members of the body of Christ. What advice would you give to a sister who confides in you, but asks you not to tell anyone, that she is being emotionally and physically abused?

7. Share some examples of what emotional abuse looks like.

8. Teenage girls are dealing with emotional and physical abuse in relationships at an early age. Suppose you are a teacher in the teen girls Bible class. How would you counsel a young girl you find out is in an abusive relationship?

9. How many times does the Bible teach we should forgive? Share Scripture(s) to support your answer.

10. Forgiveness is more for you than it is for the person who wronged you. Explain what this statement really means. What are some of the positive consequences of true forgiveness?

Chapter 5

Don't Sweat the Small Stuff

"Cookie Confusion"

"Therefore do not worry about tomorrow,
for tomorrow will worry about its own things.
Sufficient for the day is its own trouble" (Matthew 6:34).

I was on my way home from visiting a friend and decided to stop by the grocery store to pick up an item I needed. I found what I needed and headed to the checkout line. When I got in line, there was a man directly in front of me and a family of three was in front of him checking out. The family included a little boy and his mom and dad.

Sitting right next to the register was a basket of huge individually wrapped cookies. The little boy was having his way with the cookies. He took one of them, broke it into pieces and left it in the basket. This didn't sit well with the man standing in front of me. In fact, he got angry at the boy and his parents. He got so angry that he unleashed a wave of harsh words on the boy's parents because they didn't stop their son from breaking the cookies. The man turned around and tried to pull me into the conversation. He wanted me to agree with him that the parents were wrong for not chastising the child for breaking the cookies.

The family finished checking out and walked away. As they walked out of the store, the man yelled harsh words at them. The man was now next in line, and as he was being checked out, he continued to push the issue with the cashier. He tried to pull her into the issue and get her to agree that the little boy would someday end up in some juvenile detention center, and the cookie incident was only the beginning of something bigger. The man had gotten himself all worked up over the cookie incident.

The man finished checking out and went out the door. I only had one item to purchase and was checked out in less than a minute. I got my item and headed out the door. When I got outside, the first person I saw was the man who was stressing over the cookie. There was a table set up outside where a group was selling barbecue. The man was at the table talking to the person who was sitting there. I said to myself, "I'll bet he's telling that person about the cookie incident in the store." I was exactly right. As I got closer, I heard the man telling the person about the cookie incident. He was going on and on about the little boy and his parents. The man was so obsessed with the broken cookie until it had totally consumed him, and he wanted to talk about it to anyone who would listen. It was just eating him up. It was surprising to see him carrying on like that. If I could do it all over again, I would tell him, "Sir, don't sweat the small stuff!"

The Small Stuff You're Sweating

Don't sweat it! Don't worry about it! It's no big deal! You're stressing over nothing! Have you heard these words before? Would you admit that you spend unnecessary time and energy sweating, stressing and fretting over things that really are small, petty and insignificant? They're just not significant enough to require the kind of energy you expend on these situations.

What small stuff have you allowed to consume you and steal precious time and energy? What small stuff have you allowed to ruin your day, get your blood pressure up? Did someone rub you the wrong way or say something you didn't like? Who offended you? Was it the person who didn't agree with your opinion on a particular matter? Was it the person who didn't speak to you and you thought they were ignoring you? Is it your husband who won't fix the leak under the sink and won't call a plumber? Or, maybe he pulls off his dirty socks and leaves them on the floor. Is it your co-worker who leaves the kitchen in a mess and never wipes away the sugar and coffee on the counter-top? Was it the waitress or waiter in the restaurant who didn't get your order right? What small stuff are you sweating? Is it the person who keeps calling you on the phone to tell you the same thing over and over? Is it the girlfriend who won't listen to your advice but keeps calling you with her drama? Did someone cut you off on the freeway? Are you sweating the fact that you got to your dental appointment and they wouldn't take you because you were way too late? What small stuff are you sweating? Is it the preacher who preaches too long? Is it the person who asked to borrow money again? Is it the person you always call and know they're home, but they won't answer the phone? Is it the person in your household who won't turn out the lights; the same person who drank the last of the milk, left the empty carton in the refrigerator and ate the last piece of chocolate cake? What small stuff are you sweating?

I can go on and on about the small stuff we allow to get under our skin and become a rash, a sore, like a cancer eating away at us. But one thing is for sure. If you don't learn to overcome the small stuff, you will never get anything done. Sweating the small stuff will hinder you from being productive, keep you from making progress and keep you stressed out and irritated.

The Drama Queen

Surely, you know what a drama queen is. A drama queen always has some form of drama going on in her life. On the job, she's down the hall in someone's office telling them about her boyfriend who dumped her and about the new guy she's now dating, about her neighbor she had an argument with, her girlfriend she's not speaking to anymore, the person she doesn't agree with, the person she needs to confront, and the family reunion she's not going to because she doesn't like any of her family members. When she goes out to a restaurant, she doesn't like the waiter. Or, the food's too cold. The meat's not done. The bread's not hot. The soda is flat. The coffee is cold.

It doesn't take long to detect a drama queen. Usually, it only takes a few words out of her mouth to be able to put the label of drama queen on her. She's the woman in line at the bank who gets into an argument with the teller. At the post office, she gets into an argument with the post office attendant. At home, she's always on the phone talking to somebody about somebody. She loves to gossip. She thinks she's the only one who can do anything right. She doesn't mind giving you a piece of her mind and telling you when you're out of line and what you need to fix.

If you're a drama queen, you likely live in discontentment. You're never satisfied with where you are in life. You never seem to be at peace with yourself. Discontentment seems to be a way of life. You're on your third job in less than a year. You've had some really nice guys who were attracted to you, but you always seem to find something about them you don't like. You're always in the mall. You shop and shop and shop. Your closet is filled with clothes that still have price tags on them, but you wear the same clothes over and over. It's obvious you're not shopping because you need clothes. You live in a constant state of irritability. When someone calls, you accuse them of not calling enough, of calling too much. The smallest thing irritates you, and you make it bigger than it is.

The Source of the Problem

Know that when you sweat the small stuff, more than likely, it means you have a deeper problem that has nothing to do with the petty little things you're making into a mountain. Sweating the small stuff is nothing more than a cover-up for a larger issue.

If you're like most women, you're very good at covering up and hiding issues that are going on in your life. Your home could be in turmoil; problems with your husband, your children, your health, or problems on your job. But you go into your closet, get out a nice outfit; one with the price tag still on, put on the makeup, style the hair, put on the matching shoes and handbag and walk out looking like you haven't a care in the world. And the sad part is the fact that you may very well not even realize what's happening inside of you. You think sweating the small stuff is normal, a way of life. The larger problem you're dealing with; you may have had this problem for so long until it's part of who you are, and you don't even realize you have a problem that needs fixing. If you are not careful, you could end up having a meltdown, a breakdown. What's happening inside of you is already manifesting itself in ways that are destructive and non-productive. Sweating the small stuff is a manifestation of your larger issue. If your problems are not recognized and dealt with, the manifestation will become even more destructive.

Others Know More Than You Think

Because the source of your problems are possibly so buried and hidden within, you are likely in denial of them. And when someone points them out to you, you likely see them as unfairly criticizing you. You chalk it up to them being envious and jealous of you. You think they want to hurt you emotionally. You may even call them evil. What they are saying to you seems far-fetched.

Know that it's possible for others to know more about you than you think. A person on the outside can see the larger picture. It's obvious that you're too close to the situation to see the problem. Your view is limited. But a person on the outside has a seat where they can see the big picture and can give you a full description of what they are looking at. They see you as a drama queen. Every time they meet you, no matter where it is, your whole conversation is about something dramatic going on in your life. There is never a normal conversation with you. It's always about you and the drama in your life; the people you want to confront, the people you don't get along with, the people who don't like you, the relationships you are in, and so on and so forth.

How do you change what's going on inside of you? How do you deal with the problems you're experiencing? How do you take back control of your actions and attitude?

How to Stop Sweating the Small Stuff

Admit you have a problem. It's difficult to fix a problem if you never admit there is one. Admit that you spend a lot of time sweating the small stuff, expending energy on issues that are petty and insignificant. Become conscious of what's going on inside of you. Begin examining your behavior, and start listening to yourself. The next time you get into a conversation, listen to and examine the words you speak. Make a conscious effort to speak words that are positive. *"He who has knowledge spares his words, and a man of understanding is of a calm spirit"* (Proverbs 17:27).

Start paying attention to your emotions. What are the emotions you most often feel? If you feel angry, do you know what angered you? If you are disappointed, do you know the source of your disappointment? If you are frustrated, do you know the source of your frustrations? Knowing the source of your emotions will go a long way in helping you find out why you spend so much time sweating the small stuff. When you find the source of your problems, you can take actions to deal with the sources and eliminate the problem issues in your life.

Recognize the negative energy you are generating. A negative attitude can certainly generate negative energy. When you generate negative energy, it affects not only yourself, but others. Attitudes are contagious. If you are displaying a negative attitude in your home, those who live there can be affected by this. If you're a mother and you're always sweating the small stuff; griping, whining and nagging, your children can begin to imitate the behavior you're displaying.

Also, know that your attitude can cause others to avoid you. They will make every effort they can to stay out of your presence. Friends and family members may shun opportunities to spend time in your presence because of the negative energy you generate. They know when they leave you, instead of leaving with a smile on their face, they'll leave with a heavy heart, burdened down with all of the drama you dumped on them. Negative energy and a negative attitude generate turmoil. Positive energy and a positive attitude generate peace.

Examine your relationship with God. A child of God has no business sweating the small stuff. This goes against the very nature of Christ. "*Therefore do not worry about tomorrow, for tomorrow will worry about its own things. Sufficient for the day is its own trouble*" (Matthew 6:34). That's the principle of, "Don't sweat the small stuff." As a child of God, He wants you to trust Him and reflect His nature. When your actions and attitudes display worry and stress, it could very well be an indication that you are not anchored in a relationship with God.

When you make up your mind you truly want to change, God's Holy Spirit will be there to help you, to give you the self-control you need to stop sweating the small stuff, to become whole and healthy in your mind and in your spirit. The lenses you see life out of will change and you will have a new perspective on life. Instead of seeing every situation as something negative, you'll look for the good in each situation. You'll look for the lesson, the learning. Instead of seeing people as enemies, you'll begin to see others as created in the image of God. You'll see them as wanting to help you and not harm you. You'll begin to see situations as not a big deal at all.

Seek forgiveness from persons you may have hurt. Perhaps you've hurt someone; said some things that offended someone. Now you realize it was small, petty and insignificant. It wasn't even worth it. The only purpose it served was compromising peace and ending a good relationship or friendship. As you come to understand that your past behavior has been ungodly and unnecessary, you may realize that there are those you need to ask for forgiveness. It could be your husband, your children, co-workers, or whomever. Don't allow pride to keep you from asking for forgiveness. Pride can certainly be an obstacle. It can cause you to sweep it under the rug and pretend you didn't hurt anyone. You have an obligation to go to the persons you've offended and make it right. *"Therefore if you bring your gift to the altar, and there remember that your brother has something against you, leave your gift there before the altar, and go your way. First be reconciled to your brother, and then come and offer your gift"* (Matthew 5:23-24).

Seek professional counseling. It's possible that you may need professional help to get you where God wants you to be. This may be necessary to find the sources of your challenges. If you're like many others, you may feel uncomfortable about seeking professional counseling. You may be concerned with what others might say if they know you're seeing someone for psychological help. Know that seeking the counsel of others is wise. In fact, it's a principle from the

Bible. *"The way of a fool is right in his own eyes, but he who heeds counsel is wise"* (Proverbs 12:15). Sit down with someone who is experienced, skilled and trained, someone who can go with you on a journey into your past. The issues you are dealing with could very well be rooted in a past negative environment you were exposed to, including perhaps an abusive relationship you may have lived through. Somewhere in your past, you lost touch with knowing your true value and worth, knowing that God made you in His image. A professional Christian counselor can help open up your past so you can possibly see where the roots of your issues begin. Then you can start pulling them up and cutting them off.

If you think you can work through your problems without a professional counselor, that's fine and good. Even if you don't need a professional, by all means, find someone you trust and sit down and talk to them about your attitude. Understand that it's good to get things out in the open and share with others and allow them to help you see different perspectives, different views. Find someone who is led by the Spirit of God, someone who can take the Bible, open up the Scriptures and show you a picture of what God wants you to be.

We don't always like to open up and share ourselves with others. We don't like to pull off the covers and let others see the truth of what's inside, the truth of who we are, what's there when we take off the makeup, the nice outfit, the shoes and matching handbag.

God put people in place just for the purpose of counseling you and helping you get where He wants you to be. He planted people in your pathway for this purpose. Open up and let them in. You'll probably find that they've dealt with some of the same issues you're dealing with.

Change your attitude, change the words you speak. As you do, your life will change. Not only will you change, but the people who are close to you will change. You'll see the attitudes of your husband and children change, even your friends.

Stop being a drama queen. Trade in your tiara. Trade it in for a fresh new attitude, a fresh new perspective on life. Trade it in for a new way of talking. Trade in your tiara for a gentle and quiet spirit, *"which is very precious in the sight of God"* (1 Peter 3:4).

FOR DISCUSSION

1. Let's speculate for a moment. What could be some possible reasons the man in the grocery store was so annoyed by the child's behavior?

2. Getting easily annoyed can be a sign of a deeper issue, and because the issue is not dealt with, it sets in as frustration and discontentment. Discontentment is dangerous and can lead to other destructive behaviors. Find and discuss Scriptures in Philippians 4 where Paul talks about the subject of contentment. Does contentment mean complacency?

3. Have you ever worked with someone who seemed to make your life on the job miserable? Did you ever think that this person could be dealing with a deeper issue and his or her actions and attitudes had nothing to do with you but everything to do with what they were dealing with in their personal life? Share your experience, either an on the job experience, or in another area of your life.

4. When there is a deep rooted issue, it's often difficult to face or admit the problem. Before we can properly manage or eliminate a problem, there first must be admission. What are the positive consequences of admission?

5. Perhaps you've visited someone's home and you left thinking, "That home seemed so peaceful." Well, more than likely, someone in that home has a spirit of peace and you were able to detect it. If you had remained in that environment long enough, it would likely have "rubbed off" on you! Discuss and relate this to a person who has negative energy.

6. Even when we are going through difficult personal challenges, as Christian women, we should always be mindful of our conduct, our speech and our attitude. What does Colossians 4:6 say about our speech? Give examples of what this Scripture means. Find other Scriptures that teach about the

kind of mindset, attitude and spirit we are to possess. See Ephesians 4.

7. Let's face it. Life is not always a bed of roses. We get tired, weary, annoyed, fed up, and sometimes want to give up. Real challenges come into our lives. In 1 Samuel 1, what were Hanna's challenges? Did her challenges make her a drama queen? How did she deal with her challenges?

8. Did you know that there are those who say, "Well, I've done everything else I know to do. Now I'll pray." What is the problem with this?

9. Spiritual counseling is always good when a personal challenge surfaces in our lives. However, professional counseling is also sometimes necessary. Discuss some of the positive benefits that can be associated with seeking both spiritual as well as professional counseling. How can the two work together?

10. Asking for forgiveness when you've wronged someone is not always easy. What does the Bible say we should do when we have offended someone? See Matthew 5.

Chapter 6

Face Your Fears

"The Monsters"

"For God has not given us a spirit of fear,
but of power and of love and of a sound mind" (2 Timothy 1:7).

One of the amazing things about children is the power of their imagination. While something may not seem real to anyone else, in the mind of a child, it's real.

Up until I was about four years old, my family lived in a small wood-framed, two-bedroom house. I never saw monsters when we lived in this house. That didn't happen until we moved into the new house, which was built right behind the old one. We hadn't long moved in when my great uncle passed away. I went to his funeral and that night when I went to bed, I saw a figure that looked just like him standing over my bed!

The monsters seemed to follow me when I went to spend the night with my grandmother. She lived less than a mile up the road from us. Her house sat on a beautiful piece of land, way up on a hill, and there was a huge garden behind it. She raised all kinds of vegetables. She also raised chickens, and I loved to go out with her to gather eggs the chickens would have laid. It was such a treat to find freshly laid eggs. I loved to see my grandmother take her strong hands and raise up a hen from her nest and check to see if there were eggs under her. Sometimes there were.

I always had mixed emotions about spending the night with my grandmother. I loved all of the good foods she cooked; tea-cakes that were heavenly, and she made the best fried chicken and biscuits you ever wanted to eat. She canned peaches, pears and figs and made different kinds of jellies. But, no matter how good the food was, I always knew that when nighttime came, the monsters would come, and they most always did.

Different Types of Fear

Fear describes your emotional or physical reaction to something you think is dangerous or something you think is a threat to you. You may not have had monsters visit you when you were a child, but chances are, you've experienced some kind of fear at different times in your life.

There are different types of fear. There's the fear I had as a child of monsters that seemed to haunt me in the night. There's the fear that comes when you're threatened with losing something or someone you love. If you're a parent, you can have a certain type of fear when your child doesn't make it home before curfew and you fear something has happened to them. You can also have a fear of taking on new responsibilities when faced with change or a challenge that unexpectedly comes into your life. Waiting on test results from your doctor can produce fear.

It was mid-morning when my phone rang. It was someone from the Hospital. A young man was on the other end of the line, and what he said to me went something like this. "You were here in our emergency room last week, and while you were here, we took x-rays. The x-ray of your right lung shows that there is something on that lung. We would like for you to come back so we can take another look."

That's one of the times I experienced being gripped by fear as a result of a possible medical problem. You may have had a similar experience. I didn't go to the hospital as the man requested. Instead, I called my primary care doctor. I explained the situation and made an appointment for an office visit for the following morning. When I arrived, He sent me to take another x-ray. Then I went home to wait for the phone call that would deliver the results. It was a long wait to say the least. I was relieved when I found out my x-ray was normal.

Most Common Fear

One of the worst things you can do when you're fearful is dwell on your fears. When you think and dwell on situations that cause fear, you're doing nothing more than feeding them and giving them power. The monsters didn't stop visiting me when I was a child until I stopped thinking about them and dwelling on them all day every day. When I stopped giving them attention, they lost their power to exist.

The fear we most often suffer with is a false, self-imagined emotion. Examples include fear of public speaking or fear of riding an elevator. This type of fear is an emotional reaction that's triggered in our minds based on our past experiences and present mind-set. That's not to say there's no real fear, because there is. The individual who is home when a burglar tries to enter experiences a type of fear that signals danger. Fear such as this is real and serves a purpose.

One of the most common fears is the fear of failure. Most people achieve only a fraction of what they are capable of achieving. They allow fear to rob them of most of the accomplishments God planned for them. Perhaps this is the case with you. There's an opening for a promotion on your job. However, you decide not to apply because you're afraid of the responsibility that comes with it. You have a desire to get a college degree, but you never pursue your dream because you fear you may fail. You want to start your own business, but you won't for fear you may not succeed. This is an apprehensive kind of fear. You're apprehensive about stepping out on faith and pursuing the promotion, pursuing the degree you desire, starting the business you've dreamed of starting. You lack confidence in your abilities. You're afraid you might not be able to do it. You're afraid of what others will say about you if you don't make it. You're afraid that if you fail, you'll have to face some of those same people who said you weren't good enough or said you couldn't do it.

If you want to be successful in overcoming your apprehensions, your fears, whatever you're apprehensive about, do it anyway. Even though you may feel fear, face your fears. Also, don't be afraid of making mistakes. Mistakes are going to happen, and you can't avoid them. Learn the proper way to handle mistakes, and realize that they don't have to be something permanent, carved in stone; something that can't be improved. When you make a mistake, don't take it personally. See your mistakes as opportunities to learn, opportunities for growth. If success is what you desire, don't give up. Be persistent and try different approaches in order to work through your fears and get the results you desire.

Fear and Excuses

If you are fearful, you will likely make all kinds of excuses for not doing what you really desire to do. Excuses are not real reasons. You make excuses when you want to conceal reality. You'll say things like, I don't have time to go to school. I'm waiting for the economy to get better before I look for a better job. I'm waiting till I pay off some bills before I do this. I need to lose weight before I do that. I need to save some money before I do this. When my health gets better, I'll do that. These could simply be excuses you make instead of admitting you're fearful. When you are fearful of failure, fearful of not being accepted, of not being favored, of not being successful, you can come up with all kinds of excuses.

Fear and Isolation

If you're a person who walks in fear, be careful. You could start isolating yourself from others. *"A man who isolates himself seeks his own desire; he rages against all wise judgment"* (Proverbs 18:1).

When fear is present, you believe there is always something at stake, something to lose. It could be your ego, your image. You may feel that if you fail at something you desire to accomplish, perhaps your image will be tarnished. The fear in this thought can cause you to cut yourself off from others, pull away and disassociate.

When you find that you're isolating yourself from others out of fear, you are way too concerned with what others think of you. Others can indeed cause your level of self-confidence to fall. If you have a problem with holding on to your self-confidence in the face of others, you don't have to isolate yourself from them. Simply be selective about who you share the vision for your accomplishments with. It's a fact that not everyone will share in the joy of your vision, and others may not encourage you. You may hear things like, "I don't know why you want to start your own business. Are you sure you know what you're doing?" If your level of self-confidence has been damaged due to words spoken by others, examine these perceptions and replace them with the truth of who you are. Pray that you can let go of those false perceptions. No matter how much the enemy wants to make you believe otherwise, if what you desire is in God's plan for your life, you can achieve it. God made you in His image, and you should see yourself as He sees you, from His perspective. Instead of becoming a loner and isolating yourself from others because of false perceptions, love them, love yourself, and know that God has given you everything you need to accomplish the things in life He wants you to accomplish, and as long as you battle with fear and it's keeping you from pursuing God's vision for your life, you are rejecting that vision.

Replacing Fear with Faith

One of the best ways to get rid of your fears is to face them. When you face your fears, they lose their power to exist. Facing them means acknowledging them. It means bringing them out in the open, into the light where they can be exposed. One way of doing this is by sharing with a friend. When you sit down with a friend and share your fears, you're bringing them out in the open where they can't survive. They begin to lose power as soon as they're exposed.

I like to use olive oil. I like to cook with it, and I also use it in a mixture with other ingredients to make a conditioner for my hair. I learned that olive oil and some other oils lose their health benefits when they're exposed to light and air. It's recommended that olive oil be stored in a dark place to keep it from being exposed to the light. Think of your fears as being like olive oil. When they're exposed, they lose their power.

Although fear has many faces, all of them have one thing in common; they hinder you from living your best life. When you experience a fearful situation, it can affect you for the rest of your life. For example, because you had a negative experience on an airplane, you are now afraid of flying. Or, because you forgot part of your speech in front of an audience, now you're afraid of public speaking. If you are ever faced with these same situations again, just remind yourself that you have nothing to fear. Just because you had one negative flight experience doesn't mean all of your flying experiences will be negative. Just because you had one negative experience behind the microphone doesn't mean that your public speaking career is over.

When you have fearful experiences, emotions from that experience are recorded in your subconscious mind. Those emotions become imprinted onto the hard drive of your mind, and once something is imprinted, it's difficult to erase. Whenever you are faced with a similar situation, your brain can automatically replay the response from the negative experience. When it's time to get on a plane, the emotions from the negative experience you previously encountered on a plane can be replayed. When you are faced with a public speaking engagement, negative emotions from the negative experience you had at a previous engagement can very well be replayed.

Unfortunately, it's difficult or almost impossible sometimes to override the replaying of negative embedded recordings. The subconscious mind is very powerful. You have to be very careful what you say because your subconscious mind may record what you say or think, even if you don't mean it. The best way to erase negative recordings is to start saying positive words on the subject and thinking positive thoughts. For example, "I want to feel comfortable and peaceful when I'm flying." Do not say the word *afraid*! Try to keep from saying things like, "I'm not afraid of flying." While that may sound positive, your mind might decide to only pick up and record the word afraid. Stay away from negative words! Use positive self-talk to help cleanse your mind of negative emotions that create false fear.

One of the most encouraging scriptures in the Bible reminds us that fear is not something that comes from God. "*For God has not given us a spirit of fear, but of power and of love and of a sound mind*" (2 Timothy 1:7). When you know something is not inspired by God, it should be easier to take your energy out of it. God inspires a spirit "of love and of a sound mind."

Faith is a key element in overcoming your fears. To have faith is to have a belief, a conviction that fear will not control you. The

Spirit of God controls you. When faith is present, you'll step right over fear. Instead of saying, "I can't do it," you'll say, "It's already done." If you want to increase your faith, increase the time you spend in God's presence. Spend time in His word. Faith is a by-product of this. The Bible says, *"So then faith cometh by hearing, and hearing by the Word of God"* (Romans 10:17). As you draw closer to Him, He'll draw closer to you. As your experiences in Him grow, so will your faith.

Have the courage to do something you're normally afraid to do. Step out on faith and apply for that promotion even though you may be apprehensive. Go ahead and accept the offer to teach that Sunday school class. You can do it, and the more you do it, the more comfortable and in control you will feel.

Know that when you live with fear, you are living outside of God's will for your life. Unless you overcome your fears, your work in God's kingdom will be limited. The gifts and talents God blessed you with may never bring the fruit God intended. But when you face your fears, expose them and overcome them, you can live the life God created you to live.

FOR DISCUSSION

1. Read 2 Timothy 1:7. Look up the word "power." Power can have different meanings. What is the nature of the word "power" in the context of this Scripture? Discuss the difference in this type of power, and power that's motivated by control.

2. In reference to 2 Timothy 1:7; power, love and a sound mind work together to overcome fear, and there can be no substitutions. Even in our churches, we often seem to forget that there's a certain power that comes from God. When we try to substitute the type of power that comes from God, and seek to use the type of controlling power that comes from the world, or we try to operate in power, leaving out love and a sound mind, what are the consequences?

3. In childhood, what persons, places or things were you afraid of? Share your experiences.

4. In the life you now live, what is your greatest fear?

5. Discuss how fear can rob us of opportunities that would clearly translate to blessings in our lives, such as fear of public speaking can rob us of a life of publicly sharing and encouraging others, or fear of needles can rob us of a rewarding career in the field of healthcare. What are some other examples?

6. What are the positive consequences of opening up and sharing our fears with others? See ideas on page 77.

7. Faith is a key element in overcoming fear. In fact, the goal is to turn fear into faith. Discuss ways to increase faith. Include supporting Scripture(s).

8. An illness, or simply waiting on test results, can bring on stress and anxiety. Read Mark 5:25-34. Discuss this passage of Scripture, particularly the magnitude of faith this woman had.

9. The mind is powerful and plays a huge role in holding on to fears that are totally false. Unfortunately, when we have a negative experience leaving us with negative emotions, our subconscious mind records the experience, including all of the negative emotions that come with it, and whenever we are in a similar situation, the experience gets replayed in our mind and those old emotions resurface. Discuss ways we can help erase these negative recordings from the mind. Refer to Scriptures such as Colossians 4:6, Philippians 2:5, Proverbs 4:23 and others.

10. Fear can cause us to make all kinds of excuses for not doing what we know we should do. Read 1 Samuel 25. What Scripture shows that it was obvious Abigail was confident and not interested in wasting time being fearful? Abigail could have made excuses and not answered the call to do a good work. What excuses could Abigail have made had she not chosen to show courage?

Chapter 7

Live From the Inside Out

"Slow Down"

"Keep your heart with all diligence,
for out of it spring the issues of life" (Proverbs 4:23).

It had been a busy morning, and even after getting out of bed two hours earlier than I normally did, I still had a long list of things to do. After deciding I needed to get my errands out of the way, I grabbed my purse and keys, then headed out the door and into my garage. I got into my car and after taking a deep breath, I started the engine and got ready to back up. But, while I thought I put the car in reverse, I actually put it in drive. Before I realized what I had done, I pressed the accelerator! Thank God, I was able to hit the brake before I crashed through the wall of my garage.

That was just one of the experiences that let me know I needed to make some changes in my hectic lifestyle. Not only had I almost crashed through the wall of my garage, but not long after, there was another warning sign.

I was scheduled to take an elderly friend to the hospital for a medical procedure. On the day before her appointment, I reminded her several times that she had an appointment and I would pick her up at eight-thirty the next morning. I knew how forgetful she was.

In fact, I kept a calendar of her appointments so she wouldn't have to try to keep track of them.

The next morning, I woke up early because there were several things I wanted to do before I headed out to pick up my friend. I needed to fax some documents, pack a lunch because I figured I'd be at the hospital all day, and I had an errand I wanted to run before I picked her up.

After rushing to get everything done, I made it to my friend's house around nine o'clock. I was running a little late. Her appointment was for nine-thirty, and my plans to get her there early weren't working out too well. I rushed her out of the house and we left.

When we got to the hospital, I let my friend out in front and instructed her to wait for me in the lobby. When I got inside, we hurried onto the elevator and up to the outpatient surgery floor. A nice attendant greeted us with a smile and offered to assist. I gave her my friend's name. After flipping through the pages several times, the attendant asked, "Would you repeat her name please?" After I answered, she proceeded to flip through her chart looking for the name. Then she asked, "What's her date of birth?" I answered. She continued to flip through her papers looking diligently for my friend's name. Then right at that moment, something happened in my brain. An image of the calendar where I had written down the appointment was clearly visible in my mind. The date was so clear. I realized I had made a mistake.

If I had not been trying to do so many things that morning, I would have realized that it was not my friend's surgery date. I said to the attendant, "Would you please, if you don't mind, look at your schedule for tomorrow?" She looked at the schedule for the next day, and there was my friend's name. I said, "Well, I guess we'll be back tomorrow. I'm so sorry. I got the dates mixed up."

I could not believe what I had done! I was a day ahead of myself. My friend could have slept a little longer that morning, and so could I. I thought about how I rushed around trying to get everything done, packing my lunch, preparing to stay at the hospital all day. I wanted to kick myself! But I didn't. I simply said to myself, "You need to slow down!"

Heed the Warning Signs

It didn't take much for me to recognize the problem, and it's a problem many women suffer with. My mind and body were disconnected. They were not working together. Instead, they were on different frequency levels. My mind was in one place, and my body was somewhere else.

Your mind is the place from which you create life. *"Keep your heart with all diligence. For out of it spring the issues of life"* (Proverbs 4:23). Everything you do in life begins with a thought that's produced in your mind. If the mind is not healthy, the decisions you make from the mind may not be healthy. When your mind is filled with constant thoughts and mental chatter, it affects your ability to think clearly and make good decisions.

Nearly crashing through the wall of the garage and getting my friends surgery date wrong were not my only warning signs. There were others. Isn't it true that we don't always heed warning signs? Many times, instead of taking precautions after we get those signs, we ignore them. We wait until something happens, then we take precautions.

If you don't think it will happen to you, know that it will. You may not be guilty of taking your friend for surgery on the wrong date, but I'm sure you've received your fair share of warning signs. What about when you tried to answer the door when really, it was your phone ringing? Or, remember when you went to run an errand and forgot where you were going? What about the time you were looking for your keys while all the time, they were in your hand. And what about this one? You got to work and noticed you had on different shoes.

Detoxify Your Mind

You've likely heard of detoxifying the body. Detoxification of the body is the process by which the body eliminates waste. If your body doesn't go through the process of detoxification, it will become toxic and susceptible to different types of diseases and illnesses. Perhaps in your quest to get healthy, you've found yourself in your local health food store in search of cleansing products. The shelves are filled with colon cleaners, liver cleansers, total body cleansers and other detoxification products. Well, just as you have a concern for detoxification of the body, detoxification of the mind is just as important in the process of living a healthy life.

The best and most effective way to detoxify the mind is to put brakes on your mind and stop yourself from constantly thinking. How often do you stop, tell your mind to be still, and just enjoy being in the moment? How often do you stop thinking and bring your mind back to home base for a rest? And, what about when you're having a conversation with someone? Are you there in the conversation, or is your mind outside your body wandering around while the other person is talking to you? Start taking notice of yourself when you're in a conversation, and see how many times you find yourself outside of the conversation participating in mind wandering. When you're performing a task, whether it's cooking dinner or driving your car, do you give your full attention to what you're doing, or is your body operating on autopilot while your mind is gone off somewhere else? For most people, being in the present moment is something they never experience, and for those who do, it's only for short moments.

When you're driving to your destination from day to day, your mind is likely rarely fully engaged in the process of getting you from point A to point B. In fact, you may even hold a conversation on your cell phone the entire time you're driving. It's impossible to hold a conversation on the phone and at the same time be fully in the moment. Actually, it's your subconscious mind that gets you where you're going. Your conscious mind is holding a conversation on the phone as you drive. You have no recollection of what you passed, how fast or slow you were driving, how many traffic lights you drove through, nor anything else that happened along the way. You were totally unengaged in the process that got you from point A to point B.

There are many practical ways of bringing your mind back inside. Many believe that the only time the mind should be still is when you're sleeping. Stilling the mind is not something you do only at night when you're sleeping, or when you find an opportunity to take a nap. It's something you have opportunities to do all day. When you're waiting in traffic, instead of thinking, just sit there, focus inward and enjoy the moment. When you're waiting in line at the grocery store, at the bank, at the cleaners, at the courthouse, at the dentist's office, at the doctor's office, or wherever, instead of focusing outward, focus inward and enjoy the moment. Whatever task you are doing, pay attention to what you are doing. Engage yourself in the process instead of focusing so much on the end result. And by all means, don't always try to multitask. It's nice to be able to do ten things at once. But you will do your mind much good when you focus on doing one thing at a time.

Focusing inward doesn't mean you have to totally block out everything that's happening around you. It simply means don't give all of your focus to the outside. Keep some inside. If you find focusing inward to be challenging, there are several things you can do. One thing that helps me focus inward is taking a few deep breaths while focusing on each breath. This usually helps me calm my mind and pull my focus inside. I also try to find time to meditate, which is an excellent way to calm the mind. To meditate is simply to quiet the mind and focus inward.

If you're like most people in today's day and age, you own a computer. If so, you're likely familiar with computer anti-virus software. Getting quiet and focusing inward acts as sort of an anti-virus software for the mind. Anti-virus software is a product that's loaded onto a computer to protect it from viruses. I once had an experience where a virus invaded my computer. Most times when I turned on the computer, the virus would shut it down. On those rare occasions when I could get on, as soon as I started working, crash. The virus would shut the computer down. This went on for days as the virus acted like a mad monster. I called friends who gave me advice and told me to do this and do that, but nothing worked. I even called a computer expert and the instructions he gave didn't remove the virus. It seemed like I would be stuck with this virus.

Had I had anti-virus software loaded onto my computer, the ugly virus would have been stopped before making it onto my hard drive. But instead, I was always concerned with buying accessories like a new DVD burner, or a new printer or monitor to attach to it, or new speakers. I failed to realize that the heart of my computer needed my attention, needed my focus much more than the attention I was giving to the outside. It doesn't matter how many bells and whistles I attach to the outside of my computer. If the virus is in control of the hard drive, I can't listen to the new speakers, can't use the monitor, nor can I use the DVD burner and printer.

When antivirus software is loaded onto the hard drive, it constantly scans the computer for viruses. The software watches the computer, and as long as this software is watching the hard drive, the computer is protected from viruses. If a virus sneaks in, the software immediately stops it, quarantines it and renders it harmless.

Every time you take an opportunity to quiet your mind, you're activating your mind's anti-virus software. The more you bring your mind back inside your body for stillness and quiet moments, the more protection you are providing for your mind. When your mind is full from all of the thoughts you fill it with each day and tired from racing from one thought to another, it needs time to slow down and collect itself. When your mind is focused inward and resting in peace, something amazing happens. Channels in your mind open up and provide opportunities for you to gain insight into something you've been trying to figure out. It opens channels so answers you've been looking for can flow through, so wisdom can flow inside of you. When you slow down and bring your focus inward, you're opening yourself up to receive.

Manage Your Emotions

Cleansing and protecting the mind is good for the emotions. A healthy mind produces healthy emotions and manages negative emotions. God made women to be emotional in nature, much more so than men, and therefore, we feel our emotions on a deeper level than they do. We rely on our emotions more so than men. We allow ourselves to experience our emotions more than they do. We cry more than they cry. How often do you hear a man say, "I've just been on an emotional rollercoaster all day long?" Never. You likely never hear men say things like this. But, it's not uncommon to hear this from a woman. Some days, we do feel like we're on an emotional rollercoaster.

Usually, when negative emotions began to flow, they have to be released. How do you release your emotions? Perhaps it's through tears, talking it out with someone, or even eating. When I start to feel emotional stress, I like to read. I like to grab a good book or magazine and lose myself in it. Suppressing your emotions can be unhealthy. For example, you had a negative experience when you were younger. Perhaps you were abused in some way, and all of the negative emotions that came along with this abuse are still pent up inside. You felt it was better to keep it inside, so you never dealt with the situation. Ignoring or suppressing emotions can lead to greater health issues. Negative emotions are carried deep down inside and are sometimes carried for years. Perhaps you struggle with building relationships. It could very well be because of the emotions you've suppressed for so long. And, what generally happens is, when you have emotions inside that you have not allowed to be released in ways that are healthy, at some point, an explosion happens. You lose control, and your emotions are released. And usually, the thing that sets you off is something very small, very minor. Someone might have taken the Coke you put in the refrigerator. Your husband might have left the cap off the toothpaste, or left the toilet seat up. Or someone could have said something meaningless that set you off. It's usually these small things that set us off when we've spent time suppressing our emotions. And when this happens, it doesn't take long to figure out there's a bigger issue that needs to be dealt with. And if that issue isn't properly dealt with, there will be an even greater effect. When the mind is healthy, it's better equipped to transcend negative emotions and transform them into something positive and productive.

When you begin to practice living from the inside out, your life will change. Your mental and emotional states will be stronger and healthier. Begin making small steps toward taking back your mind from the outside. As you practice this, you will find yourself learning to better control your mind, better able to control the constant thinking and mind chatter that constantly goes on in the mind. You'll begin to use your mind more productively.

FOR DISCUSSION

1. As women, we can sometimes be good about going for our preventative annual physical exams, including mammograms, dental and eye exams. But we don't seem to take the same preventative care when it comes to our mental health. Give examples of experiences you've had that let you know you need to take better care of your mental health, such as not recognizing you were wearing two different shoes.

2. Give Scriptures that are key in teaching us why it's important to protect the mind. Start with Proverbs 4:23.

3. Would you agree that before we experience a physical or mental setback, we receive warning signs or red flags? What do we generally do when we receive these warnings?

4. Look up the meaning of the word detoxify, and share what this word means as it relates to the body. Give examples of healthy ways to detoxify the body, and tell why it's important to do such. Consider making this a group exercise, using the Internet to do research.

5. Detoxifying the mind is just as important as detoxifying the body. On pages 84-88, the author gives ideas that are helpful in detoxifying the mind. Share which ideas you are willing to commit to.

6. You've heard it said many times, "Women are emotional in nature." That's true. We carry our emotions deep inside, and if we don't find ways to release negative emotions, we could find ourselves dealing with negative consequences. What are some healthy ways you've discovered that are good for releasing negative emotions?

7. Read I Corinthians 6:19-20. Discuss any feelings of urgency you may feel, as well as any other emotions after reading these two verses.

8. With everything the world has to offer in the form of media, including movies, music videos, television, billboards, Internet, social media, magazines, etc., we have to be careful of what we allow into our minds, and what we allow into the minds of our children. Share ways you have found to filter what goes into your mind as well as the minds of your children.

9. It's not easy to stop all of the mental chatter that takes place in our mind. We are always thinking about something. Try this exercise. Close your eyes and focus on nothing but your breathing. How long can you do this until your mind starts to wander and you start thinking about something? Try this exercise daily and before you know it, you'll increase the time you are able to focus.

10. A sister comes to you, confides in you and shares with you that she is overwhelmed with work, overwhelmed with responsibilities at home, hasn't slept in two nights and feels like she may break at anytime. Get together with the person next to you and put together a plan of action for this sister. Be sure to use Scriptures in your counseling agenda.

Chapter 8

Be a Peacemaker

"It Was a Set Up"

*"Now the fruit of righteousness is sown in peace
by those who make peace" (James 3:18).*

I must have been in fifth grade or so. It seemed like every day girls
on the bus would fight, mostly in the evening when we were on
our way home. We lived way out in the country, so the ride home
was long. There was plenty of time for kids to get into arguments
and have a fight or two in the back of the bus. I always sat close to
the back so I never missed any action.

It was always the same girls who seemed to get into fights. On
this particular day, school had ended, and we were standing in line
waiting to board our bus. Just as I was about to board, one of the
girls came up from behind me. Her name was Edna. She said to me,
"When you get on the bus, I want you to give this candy bar to Dora."
That's all she said, then she got in line behind me. Of course I wasn't
going to refuse her, nor was I going to say anything but, "Okay." This
was one of the girls who had been in fights in the back of the bus.

We climbed onto the bus and inched our way toward the back. I
could see Dora as I got nearer to her. I really didn't think much about
handing her the candy bar. After all, it was just a candy bar. Why
would I think anything of it? Dora was sitting to my left as I smiled

at her and reached out to hand her the candy bar. Just as she took it out of my hand, Edna, who was following close behind me, reached right over my shoulder and snatched the candy bar out of Dora's hand and said, "That's my candy bar!" And before I knew it, I had been shoved out of the way and Dora and Edna had a bus fight that would rival any fight I'd ever seen. As I watched, all I could think was, "The candy bar was nothing more than a setup."

Pursuing Peace

The memory of the incident on the bus has stayed with me. I was never a person who promoted strife and disharmony. In fact, I was pretty quiet, reserved and kept to myself. So being part of something that ended so brutally really didn't sit well with me. I was thankful Dora was mature about the situation, understood that it was a setup and didn't come after me.

The American Heritage dictionary describes a peacemaker as, "Someone who makes peace, especially by settling disputes." Being a peacemaker is one of the highest honors I believe you can accomplish. How good are you at settling disputes, or creating peace out of a heated situation? Perhaps you are the person on your job everyone calls on to settle a dispute. Do you have that kind of on-the-job reputation? Perhaps you work on a job where you interact with customers, and they're not always friendly. In fact, there may even be times when you just want to "let them have it." But instead, you keep a peaceable attitude. You bite your tongue and just "hold your peace."

There are people who seem to naturally have that peaceable spirit. They have that gentleness about them, and it's not a front. They have that same spirit every time you meet them, no matter the time or place.

One of the most encouraging stories in peacemaking can be found in the Bible. It's the story about Abram, whose name was later changed to Abraham. He settled a family dispute. No doubt, you're familiar with family disputes. They're quite common in many families. The Bible says, *"And there was strife between the herdsmen of Abram's livestock and the herdsmen of Lot's livestock. The Canaanites and the Perizzites then dwelt in the land"* (Genesis 13:7). Abram responded with a peaceful resolution. *"So Abram said to Lot, Please let there be no strife between you and me, and between my herdsmen and your herdsmen; for we are brethren"* (Genesis 13:8).

We live in a world where there's always a war going on in any given moment in time. One country against another isn't the only kind of war being waged. Wars are waged in the home, husband against wife. Children acting as bullies declare verbal and even physical war on other innocent children. In the community, there are gang wars. Even in the church, members war against each other. While the weapon of choice may not always be an AK-47, much hurt and destruction can be done. If only individuals were more like Abram and simply said, *"Please let there be no strife between you and me,"* the world would be a more peaceful place.

The Work of the Holy Spirit

The greatest obstacle to peace is living without the power of the Holy Spirit. One of my greatest lessons in the work of God's Holy Spirit is in the work He did in my father. My dad was a man who worked hard and was a great provider. However, in his early years as a husband and father, at times, he was aggressive and even verbally abusive. I can remember times when I would lie in bed at night, frightened, wanting to go to sleep so I wouldn't have to listen to him, praying that he would calm down, stop yelling and go to sleep. I played a game. When he would stop yelling, I would slowly count: one, two, three, four, five, and so on, seeing how far I could count before he started yelling again. If he started back, I would have to start all over from number one. Sometimes I would make it all the way up past fifteen or twenty, thinking, that's it. He's done. But most of the time, he'd just start back yelling. And while he never physically abused my siblings or me, we were extremely intimidated by him. One thing was for sure. I couldn't change my dad and neither could my mom. However, the Holy Spirit can change anyone.

I can still remember when my father started to mature and act more in control of his actions and words. It wasn't something that happened over night. It was a process that lasted years, and as I look back over those years, I know it was the Spirit of God who changed him. My mother was a strong Christian woman, and she raised my siblings and me up in the glory and admonition of the Lord. The Holy Spirit dwelt in our home, in our mother, and in us. He had full access to my dad, changing him, making him more of what God wanted him to be. My father died a peaceful, loving man in the Lord.

Resolving Conflicts

An unresolved conflict is an obstacle to peace. When something is unresolved, it's left hanging, left dangling in the air. Walking away from a conflict without coming up with a peaceful resolution is dangerous and leaves room for negative emotions to take full control of the parties involved.

Perhaps you've experienced getting into a heated disagreement with someone, and the two of you walked away without making peace and settling it. There can be ongoing consequences to this type of situation. Every time you see the person involved, it's going to be an awkward situation. Even if the two of you are polite to each other, the memory and pain of the situation will always surface and the tension between the two of you will remain. If at all possible, when conflicts arise, settle them, and do it in a timely manner. When you get into a heated conversation or situation, it's all right to take time to cool off, or take time to think about your emotions and about what you want to say. But by all means, don't take too long. If you wait too long, the enemy just might convince you that things are all right, and you don't need to do a thing. Settle the situation. Make peace with the person.

Perhaps you've been in a situation where you responded out of anger and lost control. Or, maybe you said something to someone that was ungodly. Maybe your actions were ungodly and caused harm to someone. At any rate, you offended someone. If this is the case, you owe an apology, and the Lord expects you to offer such. *"Therefore if you bring your gift to the altar, and there remember that your brother has something against you, leave your gift there before the altar, and go your way. First be reconciled to your brother, and then come and offer your gift"* (Matthew 5:23-24).

These are biblical instructions on how to bring peace in a situation where you offended someone. The Scriptures make it clear that whatever you have to offer to the Lord is no good until you make peace with the person you wronged. And, be careful of the attitude you take with you to make peace. When you go to apologize, do it in the right spirit. If you don't, you may as well not apologize.

The world needs more peacemakers. Be a peacemaker in your home, on your job, in your community and even in your church. Be the person who calms the situation, the person who knows the value of peace and will make sacrifices to achieve peace. *"Pursue peace with all people, and holiness, without which no one will see the Lord"* (Hebrews 12:14). *"Depart from evil and do good; seek peace and pursue it"* (Psalm 34:14).

FOR DISCUSSION

1. We live in a world where peace is not always respected. Homes are broken into and individuals wreak havoc on families resting peacefully in their homes anytime of the day or night. If we're not careful, we'll find ourselves without peace of mind, living in fear and being prisoners in our own homes. How do we obtain peace of mind in light of situations such as this? Give practical and spiritual examples. Refer to Ephesians 6:10-18 and other related Scriptures.

2. An unresolved conflict is an obstacle to peace. What are some consequences of an unresolved conflict? (Page 95) How much time should you allow to go by before doing your part to resolve a conflict? Give the basis for your answer, including Scripture(s).

3. We normally think of a person who is a peacemaker as someone who is quiet and gentle. Is this always the case? Share some other characteristics that peacemakers possess.

4. Recall a time when you, or someone you know, stepped up and created an environment of peace out of a situation that was about to get out of control. Perhaps you are the peacemaker on our job and can share an experience. If not, share a biblical example.

5. There is no shortage of Scriptures in the Bible on peace. Find some of your favorite Scriptures and share them.

6. In our day and time, bullying, including cyber-bullying is a huge issue in our schools. Share the definition of cyber-bullying. As a parent, what are you doing, and what are you teaching your children to make sure they are peacemakers and not troublemakers?

7. These women had strong gifts in peacemaking: Hannah in 1 Samuel 1 and Esther in the book of Esther. What did these

women do to preserve peace? Tell how they did it and why. This could be a group exercise.

8. These women had strong gifts in peacemaking: Abigail in1 Samuel 25, and the Wise woman of Abel in 2 Samuel 20. What did each of these women do to preserve peace? Tell how they did it and why. This could be a group exercise.

9. Has anyone ever wronged you and when they came to apologize, you didn't feel as if they really meant it because of a harsh tone, harsh words, or they didn't show a peaceful spirit? Discuss the importance of going in peace, with the right attitude and spirit when we go to someone to right a wrong. What are some of the consequences when this is not done in the right spirit?

10. Family disputes are not uncommon, especially when a loved one dies. Some of the nastiest fights have taken place at the funeral home prior to the funeral, or even at the funeral. How would you counsel someone who has an issue with a family member that they can't seem to be able to resolve? What Scriptures would you use?

Chapter 9

Make Peace with Perfection

"Undoing What's Done"

"Jesus said to him, „If you want to be perfect, go,
sell what you have and give to the poor, and you will have
treasure in heaven; and come, follow Me' " (Matthew 19:21).

I had owned my part-time printing business for several years, and every time I printed a program; wedding program, funeral program, or any other kind, I always folded it myself. I was very picky about my finished products. The edges of every fold had to be perfectly even. Sometimes a customer would want a program accessory, such as a ribbon tied in a bow. Each bow had to be tied the same say, or else it had to be retied until it looked like the others.

There have been only a few occasions when I couldn't get a project completed on my own and had to invite help to come in and assist. I'm careful about doing that because on those few occasions when I invited help, I ended up redoing the work others did because it wasn't perfect. It wasn't done to my satisfaction.

I had been contracted to produce a souvenir booklet for a group who was holding a fundraiser. The booklet ended up being a nice size with lots of pages, and the customer wanted several hundred finished copies. I knew I wouldn't be able to put these together all by myself, so I pondered what to do. I decided the best thing to do was team up with one of the major printing shops in the area and allow them to use their expertise and professionalism to help me with the project. Surely, they would have no problem producing a perfect product.

It was Friday evening around six-thirty when I arrived at the printer to check on the work. They were pretty busy assisting customers, so I decided not to go behind the counter like I usually did. I could see one of the guys way in the back of the store working on my booklets, so I motioned to him to come over, and he did. I asked him how the booklets were coming along, and he said, "Everything's fine. You can come back in a couple of hours and they should be finished." I thought to myself, "This isn't so bad after all. Maybe I should contract out more business to these guys!"

It was pretty late when I arrived back at the twenty-four hour printing shop. I thought to myself, "This is working out just perfectly. I'll pick up the booklets, deliver them tomorrow morning, and the group will have the booklets right on time for tomorrow's event."

I walked into the store and went to the counter. It was empty and quiet. All of the customers who were there earlier were no longer there. The guy in the back of the store was finishing up my souvenir booklets, and another guy was boxing them. He brought one box after another to the front to be hauled out to my car.

As I stood there at the counter smiling, the cashier began to ring up my total so I could make the huge payment I owed them. As she handled her business, making sure she got my charges correct, I reached down into one of the boxes and took out one of the booklets. I opened the book, looked inside, put it down and grabbed another one. "Surely," I said to myself. "This one must be a mistake." I picked up one booklet after another and they were all the same. The booklets had been assembled wrong. The inside pages had been flipped. The page that should have been the first page was actually in the center of the booklet!

All I could think about was what a huge effort it would be to correct this mistake. I had only a few hours until delivery. Correcting the mistake meant taking all of the booklets apart, reassembling the pages, stapling each booklet together again and trimming them again. When a booklet has a large number of pages, it's necessary to trim the edges so they will be even. Trimming the booklets again was the most major problem because they had already been trimmed, and there was no more trim space. Any additional trimming would cut off words. However, if the booklets were not trimmed again, the edges would be uneven. Uneven edges! Cut off words! I couldn't bear the thought. All I could think was, "Oh my gosh! What am I going to do!"

On the next morning, for the first time, I delivered a product that was imperfect. It was a flawed product, and it took weeks, even months for me to make peace with it.

Characteristics of a Perfectionist

It doesn't bother me anymore that several of my family members and friends tell me that I think I'm the only one who can do anything right. There was a time when it bothered me, and I struggled to try and understand why I had the "I'll do it myself" attitude. But after a few times of having to redo what someone else didn't do right, or undo what someone else did wrong, or refold what someone else folded the wrong way, or unseal what someone else shouldn't have sealed—after a few times of that, it doesn't bother me anymore when my family and friends tell me, "You think you're the only one who can do anything right." They tell me I'm a perfectionist.

While my family and friends call me a perfectionist, I have to disagree. There are some personality traits a perfectionist has that I don't have. Now, I will admit, I can get pretty bent out of shape when something isn't done to my satisfaction, but that is in no way an admission that I'm a perfectionist. No, I'm not a perfectionist. I simply think that things should be done and tasks should be completed in a way that says the person who did it was paying attention and cared about the process as well as the finished product.

Do you have personality traits of a perfectionist? Do you get all bent out of shape when something isn't done to your satisfaction, or when someone does something for you and they don't do it the way you would have done it? Do you stress out and beat yourself up when you experience a failure or setback? Do you look for flaws and imperfections in your efforts and in the efforts of others instead of looking at the big picture and finding the good?

A visit to your home could reveal if you're a perfectionist. In the home of a perfectionist, one might find every spoon, fork, and knife perfectly polished and aligned in the silverware drawer. Every cup in the cabinet is perfectly placed with all of the handles turned the same way. Every canned good in the pantry is neatly stacked and organized in food category and in alphabetical order. Is this your home? If so, you check the pictures on the wall occasionally to make sure they are hanging without tilting or leaning in any one direction. No one, and I mean no one, is allowed to fold the towels and sheets when you do the laundry. No one folds your towels and sheets like you. When others pitch in and lend a hand, as soon as they're out of sight, you unfold what they folded and refold it to your satisfaction.

On the job, nothing is done right unless you do it. You even did a total makeover on the presentation your co-worker put together for a meeting. You didn't like the fonts she used. You didn't like the color of paper she printed it on. You like your headings bold. She didn't bold her headings. You are in a constant battle, a constant struggle with perfection.

These are just a few of the characteristics of a perfectionist. There are others. If you're a perfectionist, you likely set high, unrealistic standards for yourself. It's all right to set standards. There's absolutely nothing wrong with this. In fact, you should have standards. However, your standards should be realistic, and they should be attainable. When you develop standards that are unrealistic and unattainable, you are setting yourself up for disappointment. It's like planning to lose twenty pounds in one week. When you plan such unrealistic goals, you are doing nothing but planning for failure.

Attitude of Carelessness

The opposite of the perfectionist is the person who just doesn't care, and their attitude of carelessness shows in their work and in their lifestyle. Are you that person? If so, you probably couldn't care less about what your kitchen looks like. If you open the drawer where you keep the spoons, forks and knives, you may have to shuffle things around in order to find what you want. Nothing is organized. And your pantry; no organization whatsoever. When it takes you twenty minutes to find that can of cream of mushroom soup, that's not even enough to make you organize the pantry. It's totally impossible to find something when you need it. You have a load of canned goods that are outdated. Boxed and packaged goods need to be thrown out because the expiration dates are long past. There's absolutely no room to put anything else in your pantry.

Then there's the refrigerator. Very seldom does the refrigerator get cleaned out. There are containers of molded food, including a year—old carton of eggs. And, the empty milk container should have been thrown out a long time ago.

Then at work, you make no contribution to the presentation your team is putting together. You have no suggestions, no input, no thoughts or ideas. You just want them to get it done and give you a copy. You couldn't care less about the contents of the presentation. You don't care what font they used or what color paper it's printed on. Which are you? Are you the perfectionist, or are you on the opposite extreme? If you're a perfectionist, you're always worrying about something, stressing about something and anxious about something. Something is always nagging you. You're always trying to fix things, trying to make things fit inside the box you've created.

If you're on the opposite extreme you don't care much about attention to detail. The standards you set are not at all difficult to achieve. And having a neat and tidy silverware drawer or an organized pantry is certainly not at the top of your priority list.

Making Peace with Perfection

If you're obsessed with perfection, that means you are in a battle with perfection, and you'll never win. You'll never achieve the level of perfection you desire. It's unrealistic. Not only do you create stress for yourself when you demand perfection and set high, unrealistic expectations for yourself and others, but you can also make things miserable for others. Your family is probably used to your behavior by now and has likely learned to live with you. So they likely allow you to live in your self-made world. But that may not be the case with co-workers whom you are perhaps constantly at odds with because you seem to always find flaws in their efforts instead of looking at the big picture and seeing the good in their efforts. While you may see your attitude as normal, they see you as a person with personal problems and issues, and they've decided to chalk up your behavior as, "She's just someone with issues."

It's possible that your efforts to achieve perfection are simply a part of who you are. You may not know why you do these things. In fact, you may not even like exhibiting this behavior. You could be suffering with some type of compulsive disorder and you're not aware of it.

Compulsive behavior produces a cycle of anxiety. You seek to relieve the anxiety with more compulsive behavior. However, you feed the cycle and it continues. When you can't stand having a canned good out of place, and you make multiple trips to the cabinet to make sure everything is where it should be, you're feeding your compulsive behavior. Keep in mind that some compulsive behaviors require professional help to overcome.

In order to make peace with perfection, you must realize that perfection is impossible. It's all right if a canned good gets out of alphabetical order in the cabinet. That's not something to put your family on lockdown for. And, by all means, it's not necessary to unfold and refold sheets and towels folded by others. Try it. The next time it happens, just let it go and see that it's no big deal. And, stop stressing on the job over things that are just plain petty. Yield to the thoughts, opinions and efforts of your co-workers. Just because they don't like the same color paper you like, or they don't use the same fonts you use when you put together a presentation, this isn't a reason to take it upon yourself to re-do a presentation they spent valuable time putting together. Recognize that such behaviors are small, petty and serve no purpose but to compromise peace. Know that when you act out in behaviors such as these, you are minimizing the efforts of others and putting your wants and desires before theirs.

Instead of possessing the attitude of a perfectionist, start engaging in behavior that promotes calmness, not anxiety. Engage in behaviors that promote unity, not division, peace, not strife.

FOR DISCUSSION

1. What is a perfectionist? What might be some of the causes of a person having the attitude of a perfectionist? God allowed the author to go through the process of delivering an imperfect product to a client. What lessons should she have learned from this?

2. God doesn't expect us to be perfect in and of ourselves. How do we know this? Find Scripture(s) to support your answers.

3. What is a characteristic of compulsive behavior? Describe some compulsive behaviors. Do research and determine what might be some of the causes of compulsive behaviors. This could be a group exercise.

4. While it's good to have standards and expectations, it's not wise to set them so high that they are out of reach, as would be the case for a young woman who sets high, unrealistic standards and expectations for a marriage partner. If we were to evaluate her list we might think, "She wants someone perfect." What are some of the consequences of setting unrealistic standards and expectations for individuals such as: (a) a marriage partner, (b) our children, and (c) people on the job and in the church?

5. Suppose a young lady shows you her list of expectations for a marriage partner and asks for your opinion. After examining her list, your first thought is, "She'll never find him. She wants someone perfect." What would your response to her sound like? Make a list of things you would advise her not to compromise on.

6. One of the consequences of setting our standards too high for a marriage partner is, we get frustrated when we can't find perfection. We get tired of waiting and we accept what we get, thinking we can change the person and transform

them into what we want them to be. Discuss the mental, emotional and physical consequences that come along with this marriage, for both husband and wife.

7. A person who has the attitude of a perfectionist not only sets high, unrealistic standards for others; they do the same thing for themselves. They measure themselves by their accomplishments and because they are overly critical of themselves, cannot emotionally cope when they don't accomplish their goals. This can lead to a place of emotional darkness. What is one of the most destructive consequences of being overly critical of self and why?

8. Setting high expectations for self can affect all areas of life. It's not uncommon to find a sister who might not invite others into her home to visit and fellowship because her home is not spotless, dustless, clutter free and perfect. If you had the opportunity to encourage this sister, what would you say? What Scriptures would be good to help her recognize that there's a higher good to be served, and God's work and will takes precedence over her unjustified insecurities. Find Scriptures that teach us to look out not just for ourselves, but also for the interests of others; Scriptures that teach us to be hospitable, be forgiving of self and others and any other Scriptures that might come to mind.

9. While we in the flesh will never achieve perfection, each day, we should strive for a life of perfection as we walk in the light of Christ. We should always be on the journey towards perfection as was Paul. Read Philippians 3:12-13. Discuss this passage of Scripture as it relates our journey.

10. God doesn't care about our unrealistic standards and expectations. God's love is perfect, and when His love is made perfect in us, we no longer have to live in anxiety and depression. We can live a life of freedom and peace. Read 1 John 4:12. According to this Scripture, what is the one thing God wants us to focus on in order to achieve His perfect love? See also Mark 12:30-31 and Colossians 3:12-14. Elaborate on these Scriptures and what they mean.

Chapter 10

Be Flexible

"Wasted Time"

"And do not be conformed to this world,
but be transformed by the renewing of your mind,
that you may prove what is that good and acceptable
and perfect will of God" (Romans 12:2).

M y husband and I were really looking forward to going to the wedding at our church. In fact, we hadn't been married very long and had only been members of this particular church for a short while. I was anticipating being in a social setting with church members where we could get to know others at the congregation. I reminded my husband a couple of times during the week that the wedding was at five o'clock on Saturday. I certainly wanted to keep it on his mind. You know how guys are, especially when it comes to going to weddings. Sometimes it can become a challenge trying to get them to attend such events.

Saturday rolled around, and finally it was time to get dressed for the wedding. Things were going pretty smoothly. My husband even seemed excited about going. We walked out of the house around four-thirty and headed to the ceremony.

The church was only fifteen minutes from the house, so we didn't think we needed to rush. As we got near the church, we could see cars parked alongside the highway. I remember thinking, "What a huge crowd." As we drove up to the church, to our surprise, we could see that the parking lot was covered with people. There were even people getting into their cars. We thought, "What's going on? It's time for the wedding to start. Why are so many people outside and why are some leaving?"

We found a parking spot and my husband got out of the car and asked someone what was going on. When he got back, he was not a happy camper. We found out that we had missed the wedding. The wedding was at four o'clock, not five o'clock, and the people were leaving to go to the reception hall.

I can't describe the humiliation and stupidity I felt. It was certainly my fault. I should have looked at the invitation to confirm the time, but I thought I remembered it being five o'clock.

In our frustration, we made the decision to go to the reception. I remember getting to the reception and standing in a very long line with my husband. I guess we were standing in line waiting to be served. I just remember my husband being really frustrated, unfriendly and not in a good mood. I was pretty much the same. We had actually started to get on each other's nerves and probably the nerves of the people around us. Well, needless to say, we ended up getting out of line and walking out. We went home irritated and frustrated.

Practicing Flexibility

Have you ever had someone change their mind, change your plans or change the rules of the game in the middle of the game? If you've been in any of these situations, you've been in a situation where you've had to refocus, make some adjustments and get back on track.

Some people have this amazing ability to bounce back from challenging situations or adversities. No matter what challenge they face, they survive it. There's a saying that goes something like this. *"Blessed are the flexible, for they shall not be bent out of shape."*

Learning to be flexible is one of the most valuable tools you can possess. People who are flexible are survivors. They don't crumble under the weight of a challenging situation.

What would you do in the following situation? You are preparing for a very important meeting. In fact, it's the most important meeting of your career. You've prepared a really impressive Power Point presentation that you will present to your company's most important client. Not only will your client be there, so will your boss and other executives from your office. The meeting is away from the office because your conference room isn't large enough to hold everyone. The meeting will take place in the back room of a nice local restaurant.

You get to the restaurant a little later than you planned because you were putting the finishing touches on your presentation. It's time for your performance. You stand up, go to the computer and Power Point projector that was set up earlier by someone from your office, and find out you can't get the presentation up on the screen. There you are in the middle of the most important meeting of your life, and you can't get the projector to work. You give up and decide to go ahead and pass out the handouts your secretary copied and packed for you. But when you open the package, you find out your secretary made copies of the wrong presentation. What do you do?

No doubt this is a situation that requires a huge amount of flexibility, or else you will find yourself crumbling under the weight of this challenge.

What does it really mean to be flexible? Some terms that are synonymous with the word flexible include elastic, resilient, responsive to change, adaptable, able to bend, capable of withstanding stress without injury, able to undergo change or modifications. Just how flexible are you in your everyday life? How elastic are you? How resilient are you? How responsive to change are you? How adaptable are you? Are you able to bend without getting bent out of shape? Are you capable of withstanding stress without injury? There will be times when a situation will surprise you, catch you off guard, give you little to no time to think about what to do. When this happens, it's not the time to fall apart, break down, throw your hands up and say, "Whatever!" It's time for flexibility.

Not every challenge will come in an instant. Sometimes a challenge can be a slow process where you'll have time to think things through, ponder over the situation and talk it over with friends and spiritual counselors. Whether it's something that comes up in an instant, or something that allows time to think things through; either way, you need to be flexible, able to bend.

Flexing the Mind

Usually, when the word flexible is mentioned, it's in the context of the physical body. Surely you desire a flexible body that's able to bend and stretch beyond the norm. You want to be able to touch your toes and reach up to the sky. However, if your body is not flexible enough, you could strain a muscle.

One important element of flexing is relaxing. When you're relaxed, you're more flexible. Perhaps you exercise regularly. If so, you have likely learned that as you exercise and stretch your muscles, forcing them to adapt to different positions, stretching them beyond the point that you normally stretch them, relaxing is of the utmost importance. If you don't learn to relax and lean into the positions, you could find yourself straining a muscle.

That's the physical perspective on what can happen when your body isn't flexible. But just as importantly, you need to be mentally and emotionally flexible. When you're in a challenging situation where you're about to give a presentation and your Power Point projector won't work and you brought the wrong handouts, it's going to be pretty challenging to relax. But it's necessary if you want to keep from falling apart.

My husband and I couldn't handle it when we got to the wedding and it was over. This is an example of two people who were not mentally and emotionally flexible. We attempted to be flexible. That was demonstrated in our decision to go on to the reception. We wanted to be flexible and adjust and refocus. But at the time, we really weren't in good mental and emotional shape, so we didn't do a good job of being flexible. We pulled an emotional muscle, and that's why we ended up going home. That emotional injury was manifested in frustration, complaining and griping. Had we been in good emotional and mental condition, we would have relaxed, taken a deep breath, totally refocused, forgot about missing the wedding, gone to the reception, greeted the couple and had a wonderful evening.

A person who is flexible knows that inflexibility is an enemy to their personal growth. When you're not flexible, all you're doing is holding on to something that really isn't working for you. When you don't let go, there's no room for new ways of looking at things, new opportunities, new endeavors, new ways of doing things, new thoughts and ideas, new beginnings. When something comes to you, a situation or a circumstance, and you reject it by not being flexible, you could very well be rejecting a blessing God is ushering into your life, something you need to get you to the place He wants you to be.

As my husband and I have grown personally and spiritually, we're doing a better job of being flexible. And what we've found is that becoming flexible is not something that comes overnight. It's a process.

I'm reminded of what happened a few months ago when my husband planned a trip for us to go visit his grandmother. It was actually a pretty busy week for me, but because I knew how important this trip was for him, I put several things on hold and pretty much rescheduled my entire life for a couple of days so we could take this trip. But when the day we had planned to leave rolled around, he put the trip on hold.

Later that day, I had to meet a friend to drop off a package to her, and I remember telling her about how my husband had totally changed our plans at the last minute. I was going on and on about how I had rescheduled my life so we could take this trip. I remember my friend saying, "You need to be more flexible." She could tell where I was going with the conversation, and her words reminded me that I lacked flexibility. I was reminded that I needed to relax, take a deep breath, refocus, adapt and move on from that situation.

The opposite of flexible is inflexible. There will be times when you'll be faced with a situation that requires you to stand. There will be no room for flexibility, bending or compromising. Being flexible does not mean compromising your morals, principles and spiritual teachings. If you're being challenged by a situation where flexibility would require you to step outside of God's will and you're considering doing this, you're about to strain a spiritual muscle, and this will become an obstacle for you. Exercise flexibility but know when to stand!

FOR DISCUSSION

1. What does the term flexible mean? How is flexibility achieved?

2. If you are one who enjoys going to the gym to engage in physical exercise, you're likely familiar with flexibility and its benefits. Try this exercise. Stand up with your arms hanging relaxed next to the sides of your body. Relax your body. Inhale deeply. Exhale. Now slowly bend your upper body at the waist and slowly reach your hands towards your toes. Don't overdo it. How flexible are you? How close can you get to your toes?

3. Think about trees in a hurricane. Those that survive are those that are flexible and able to bend. Emotional flexibility is a wonderful quality. It means you're able to change the course of events easily or compromise in an unexpected situation. The good thing about being flexible is you bend, but you don't break. When personal storms come into your life, on a scale of one to ten, where do you fall on the emotional flexibility monitor, with one being not flexible at all and ten being extremely flexible?

4. Have you ever had an experience where you showed up for an event and it was the wrong date, or wrong time? If so, you know how embarrassing this can be. Even if no one knows, this can cause you to be pretty hard on yourself. Share your experience.

5. Being unwilling to bend can be directly related to stubbornness and pride and will end in brokenness. Consider King David when he walked out and saw Bathsheba taking a bath on the roof in 2 Samuel 11. Because of his pride and stubbornness, he was unwilling to bend, so he broke. What were his far reaching consequences?

6. While it's good to be able to bend and be flexible, there are those who are constantly bending, constantly compromising

and giving in to others. They spend so much time bending until they hardly ever stand up. Explain why this is dangerous.

7. Jesus was flexible. There were many situations where He compromised and stepped outside of the box, just as He did when He conversed with the woman at the well in John 4. And while He was flexible in some things, in one thing, for the sake of our salvation, there was no compromising. What was Christ unwilling to compromise on? Give Scriptures.

8. While it's good to be flexible. It's also good to know when to stand and not bend. Think about your lifestyle. How flexible are you when it comes to allowing certain individuals to drive your car, stay at your house, borrow money, pick up your children from school, babysit your children? Share some of those things in your life where there's just no room to bend.

9. Knowing when to bend and when to stand is directly related to our relationship with God. As Christian women, what are the spiritual keys to knowing when to bend and when to stand?

10. Being physically flexible is good for the body, mind and soul. However, physical flexibility takes sweat and effort. Do you have a physical exercise routine? If so, share your routine. Eating healthy is also important in being flexible and physically fit. What are some foods you love to eat, eat often, but know they should be eliminated from your diet or only eaten in moderation? Gather a group of sisters and each sister commit to going ten days without eating foods from this list. After ten days, you should see some improvements in your overall health.

Chapter 11

Be an In-Law, Not an Outlaw

"A Visit to the In-laws"

"Entreat me not to leave you,
Or, to turn back from following after you;
For wherever you go, I will go;
And wherever you lodge, I will lodge;
Your people shall be my people,
And your God, my God" (Ruth 1:16).

My husband and I were still newlyweds when we decided to take a trip to visit his parents. We had been married about six months. When the day we planned to leave rolled around, we packed our things, loaded up the car and headed out. It was Friday. I had worked that day and was quite tired for the journey to my in-laws. The drive was about two hours long, and by the time we got there, it was dark. When we arrived, it took all the energy I had to get inside, greet the family and find a comfortable place to rest and relax. However, my husband decided he was going to visit friends who found out he would be in town for the weekend. When he asked if I wanted to go with him, I didn't hesitate to say, "No, I just want to stay here and get some rest. You go and have fun with your friends." After he left, I took a shower, said goodnight to my in-laws and went to bed.

We ended up having a really great time visiting my husband's parents. I thought I was doing a good job of settling into the family and making myself right at home. After spending Friday and Saturday, we packed up on Sunday afternoon and headed back home.

On Monday evening following our trip, the phone rang. It was my mother-in-law. I answered the phone and greeted her. We chatted for a bit. Then I told her to hold on while I call her son to the phone. I figured she was calling to talk to him. However, she said, "I called to talk to you." So I relaxed, got comfortable and opened my ears to listen to what she had to say. My mother-in-law went on to tell me that I should not have said "no" to my husband on Friday night when he asked me if I wanted to go with him to visit his friends. She told me I should not have allowed him to go alone. I listened attentively to her, and as I listened, I thought to myself, "She has no business getting into our affairs!"

I got off the phone with my mother-in-law and pondered her words. I was really caught off guard by this. As I pondered what she said, I convinced myself that my mother-in-law had no business saying what she said to me.

A Defensive Nature

One of the main reasons it may be difficult to work through the in-law relationship is a defensive nature. It's not uncommon to find a defensive nature in the mother-in-law/daughter-in-law relationship. Unfortunately, many of the difficulties and challenges experienced in this relationship are a result of society's stereotyping the mother-in-law. She's been stereotyped as nosy, a busybody, a meddler, even deceptive. You've heard the mother-in-law jokes. You've seen the sitcoms putting the mother-in-law in a role that supports the stereotype. So when a woman gets married and she gains a mother-in-law, if she's not careful, she'll find herself, without even thinking about it, putting up her defenses. She comes into the relationship on the defensive end, ready to do battle with her mother-in-law because she automatically thinks this is going to be a challenging relationship. She goes into the relationship expecting her mother-in-law not to be any different from the mother-in-law who was created and labeled by society.

Another reason for challenges in the mother-in-law/daughter-in-law relationship is the conflict between the old and new generation. If you're a mother-in-law, perhaps you entered the relationship with certain so-called old-school expectations, but your daughter-in-law may not meet those expectations. She may have very different morals, values and principles than you. Chances are, she dresses differently from the way you dress. You wear long skirts. She may wear short skirts. She may talk differently from the way you talk. Your conversation may be soft and gentle. Perhaps hers is more frank and her words not as gentle. When it comes to managing the home, things that might be important to you may not be as important to her. You may keep a neat, clean and tidy house. She may not. You may have served up hot home-cooked meals for your son when he lived at home. She may not. You may be in church every time the doors open. She may not go as often as you. You never would have chosen a job where you would have to travel and leave your family for days at a time. She might be an aggressive career woman who doesn't mind traveling if it means advancing her career goals. You never would have left your children at a daycare. She may have no problem leaving her children at a daycare.

Sometimes a generation gap manifests itself in the form of a wall that comes up between the mother-in-law and daughter-in-law, making it extremely difficult for them to communicate. Mother-in-law wants to change daughter-in-law, and daughter-in-law wants mother-in-law to accept her for who she is. Before you know it, a power struggle develops between the two. Mother-in-law feels like daughter-in-law can't adequately care for her son. Therefore, she tries to treat him as though he's still her little boy. She calls him often to come over, pretending she needs him to fix something or look at something. She cooks his favorite meals and invites him over. Daughter-in-law feels like she's competing with mother-in-law for her husband's time and affection. Her husband stays in the doghouse because she wants him to put his mother in her place, but he refuses. He's in the middle of a tug of war between his wife and mother.

How to Tame Your Defensive Nature

When you're ready to tame your defensive nature, start by evaluating your relationship with Christ. Your relationship with Him will reflect itself in your relationship with others. The Bible is a book about relationships, and that's where you should go to find out how to conduct yourself in relationships. *"Be kindly affectionate to one another with brotherly love, in honor giving preference to one another"* (Romans 12:10). Let God's Spirit be your guide. As you walk in the Spirit, you will be compelled to overcome relationship challenges.

Overcoming doesn't mean fixing the other person. Overcoming can be as simple as being able to accept the situation for what it is, accepting a person for who they are and being willing to do your part in making the best of the situation. It can mean treating your in-law with love and respect no matter what the situation. When you walk in the Spirit, you have no desire to be part of a relationship that's bitter and unholy. Your goal is to do whatever is within your power to bring peace and harmony into your relationships. *"If it is possible, as much as depends on you, live peaceably with all men"* (Romans 12:18).

If you have a daughter-in-law, perhaps there are things you can do to make it easier for her to tame her defensive nature. You may not approve of the person your son married. She may not be the girl of your choice, but she's the girl of his choice. You may not approve of her, may not like the way she dresses, the way she talks, the way she keeps house, the profession she chose, or anything else. But it will serve you well to accept the fact that he married her, she is part of your family, she is your daughter-in-law and will likely be the mother of your grandchildren. Accept her for who she is. Focus on being the best you can be and using your godly influence to help her be the best she can be. Sometimes we're so busy fighting others with our words, attitudes and actions, until we fail to use our greatest tool to help them see a different perspective. We fail to show others the Spirit of Christ. We become so busy lifting up ourselves before them, until we fail to lift up Christ.

Any mother who genuinely loves her son will want him to be in a relationship with a wife who is happy. The happier the wife, the happier she will make her husband. When she's happy, she will please him the way he wants to be pleased. If she's unhappy, his pleasures will be limited. As a mother-in-law, when you don't respect their relationship and you're always dipping into their marriage business, uninvited, disrespecting your daughter-in-law and making her feel like she's inadequate, incapable and incompetent, you're doing a lot more harm than good. You're not only straining your relationship with her, but you're also driving a wedge between the two of them. Men can have a deep affection for their mother. It's not always easy for them to turn Mom down. It's not always easy for a son to make Mom second. As a mother, encourage your son to put his wife on a pedestal, instead of encouraging him to put you on a pedestal. Instead of hindering him in his marriage, allow him and his wife to build their marriage relationship one block at a time, learning from their mistakes the same way perhaps you did.

If you are a daughter-in-law, perhaps there are things you can do to help make it easier for your mother-in-law to tame her defensive nature. Change your attitude about the mother-in-law stereotypes. Not all mothers-in-law fit the stereotypes. Give your mother-in-law a chance to show you she can be a loving, caring mother-in-law who will allow you and your husband to build your own lives, just the two of you. Of course she's not perfect, and if she's a mother-in-law for the first time, she'll make some mistakes. She may say things she'd like to take back. Allow her to make mistakes and learn from them. Understand that this mother-in-law thing is new to her, just like being a daughter-in-law is new to you. And, don't discount everything your mother-in-law says to you. There will be times when she will have good, sound, honest advice for you, and even if it stings or hurts a little, or makes you feel uncomfortable, take it and examine it. If it's good constructive criticism, by all means take it. Instead of getting defensive, own up to it and thank her for the advice.

A Mother-in-Law's Advice

My mother-in-law passed away several years ago, and I thank God for the phone call she made to me after our weekend visit. As time went on and I grew personally and spiritually, I understood what my mother-in-law's words really meant. Since then, I've thought about our conversation many times, and even shared it with other women who are trying to build successful in-law relationships. My mother-in-law had my best interest at heart, and her words were an expression of that. She had been married for many years and knew those things that are important in marriage. She was giving me some good old advice about how to keep my husband happy, and instead of getting defensive, I should have been listening and learning. She wasn't just speaking in the context of that night. I realize now that she was talking in the context of our entire marriage. It's good when husband and wife can find time to go out and have fun together, hang out with friends together. I realize now that she was saying to me in so many words, "Sometimes you have to make sacrifices. You were tired, I know. But your husband would have loved having you with him that night when he went to meet his friends. You can't always let him go out alone. For future reference, whenever you can, go with your husband. Do things with him. He wants you with him."

When I told my husband about the phone call from his mother, at that moment, he didn't say anything. But a few days later, he said to me, "I called my mother and talked to her. I told her she doesn't have to be concerned about you going places with me."

Although that phone call my husband made to his mother made me feel cherished and protected, it didn't change the fact that my mother-in-law was right on. My husband loves it when I go with him, even if he's just going down the street to the corner store. My mother-in-law knew her son. She knew he was an affectionate person. She was only trying to share with me a little piece of him. She was trying to help me.

My mother-in-law turned out to be one of the most awesome women I will ever meet. She was a strong woman, the rock of her family, and when she passed away, a piece of all of us went with her. Be the best mother-in-law you can be. Be the best daughter-in-law you can be.

FOR DISCUSSION

1. Read Genesis 2:18-24. From these Scriptures, we can see characteristics found in marriage. What are some? Start with companionship and commitment. Discuss each characteristic and why it's important in marriage. In our day and time, statistics show that 50% of marriages end in divorce. Review the list of characteristics you made. What's missing from marriages today and how is this affecting the marriage relationship?

2. The in-law relationship can be most rewarding. If you are in a marriage relationship and your in-laws make you feel special; like you were born into their family instead of related by marriage, take a minute and share. Share qualities that make your relationship with your in-laws special.

3. In general, mothers-in-law have been unfairly stereotyped, and this has caused many brides to enter into the marriage with their defenses up. How would you counsel a newlywed who is concerned about developing a good, healthy relationship with her new mother-in-law? What Scriptures would you share with her?

4. It should always be our goal to have the best relationship possible with our in-laws. However, because we are all different, have different personalities, and come from different backgrounds, challenges and conflicts do happen. Unfortunately, it's not always possible to have the kind of relationship you desire with your mother-in-law or other in-laws. And when this is the case, as a Christian woman, there are basic characteristics you should always display, especially when you are in the presence of your in-laws. What are some of them?

5. One of the main points of contention in the mother-in-law/daughter-in-law relationship is control. It isn't always easy for a mother-in-law to let go and accept the fact that her son has a wife who is now a priority in his life. In situations such as this, it's never a good idea to engage your mother-in-law in a power struggle. What are the consequences of a power struggle between a mother-in-law and daughter-in-law?

6. One of the important elements of any relationship is being a good listener. Hearing and listening are two different things. Perhaps you hear, but you're not really listening. The author spoke of an incident where her mother-in-law gave her advice. Did the author listen? What mistakes did she make in this situation?

7. A great example of a healthy mother-in-law/daughter-in-law relationship is the relationship between Naomi and Ruth. Turn to the book of Ruth and read Ruth 1:15-17. Based on these Scriptures, make a list of the obvious characteristics of this mother-in-law/daughter-in law relationship.

8. Ruth was compelled to remain with her mother-in-law and as a result, she was tremendously blessed. In what ways was she blessed?

9. Was Ruth a good listener? Give Scriptures from the book of Ruth to support your answers.

10. Read Ruth 4:15. How did the women describe Ruth's relationship with Naomi?

Chapter 12

Weather the Storms of Life

"The Hurricane"

"He calms the storm,
so that its waves are still" (Psalm 107:29).

It had been forecasted that a hurricane would hit the Houston-Galveston area where my three siblings and I lived. Our plans were to evade the storm by traveling to our mother's house, which was about a two-hour drive. Little did we know that the storm would change its mind and instead follow us to our mother's house.

It was mid Friday afternoon when the weather forecasters confirmed that the storm would likely turn and not hit the Houston-Galveston area as had been previously forecasted. But unfortunately, this information came too late to stop the massive evacuation out of Houston that had already begun. There was chaos and confusion on every highway out of town. And before long, an evacuation notice was issued for persons living in the small town where my mother lived.

I arrived at my mother's house a day or so before my siblings, and on that Friday afternoon, she and I discussed what we should do. After watching more of the weather forecasts and seeing footage of the evacuation, including the chaos on the highways, we decided we should ride out the storm behind the walls of her house. We discussed it again when my siblings arrived and they agreed.

I remember the atmosphere that Friday afternoon before the storm. It was very calm and peaceful. My mother's house is in the country surrounded by trees, and as I sat out on the patio pondering the decision we had made to weather the storm at home, I stared at the huge pecan trees that towered over the house. Two huge pecan trees and four huge oak trees had stood for as long as I could remember. They were there long before I was born. I thought to myself, "Surely, they would never fall on us." I prayed that God would keep their roots in the ground and hold them up so that after the storm, they'd be still standing.

As I sat there, my mind went back to when we were children. I thought of how my siblings and I would play under those trees, building playhouses and mud cakes. Only pleasant memories could be associated with the trees that towered over the house. But tonight, a hurricane would threaten not only their very existence, but also ours.

The calm atmosphere slowly began to fade, giving way to the whistle of the wind. My son and his family had not yet arrived from Houston, and I was getting a little concerned. We had heard stories on the news of people running out of gas in the evacuation. I prayed that my children would make it safely. Another point of contention for me was the fact that my husband wouldn't be joining us. His job in law enforcement wouldn't allow him to leave the city.

The wind continued to pick up speed. My nephews put tape on the windows to keep them from shattering. Then they made sure nothing was left outside that was not secured. Later that evening, my son and his family finally arrived.

We spent the first few hours of the night watching television and listening to the radio. The wind continued to increase in speed and intensity. The weather forecasters warned us that the storm was headed right for our little town and we should "hunker down," as they said.

We kept track of the storm and its whereabouts, that is, until the electricity went out around midnight. Then our ability to watch television and listen to the radio ended. Our only communication was our cell phones, which we used to keep in touch with relatives in other cities who were watching the news and reporting back to us. As we sat there in the dark, my brother's cell phone rang. It was a relative calling to tell us that a house had floated away not far from our house.

We were huddled in the hallway in the center of the house. The wind roared like the sound of a train roaring down the track as it gripped the roof of our house. I could hear the roof cracking and feel the house shaking as the wind struggled to tear it off its foundation. It seemed at any moment, the roof would fly off the house. This went on for hours, and the only thing we could do was pray and wait. Oh, how I longed for that night of terror and fear to come to an end.

By the grace of God, we made it through that night alive. The next morning, as we opened the door to assess the damage, as far as we could see, the ground was like a river, covered with water brought by the hurricane. From a distance, we could see huge trees lying on the ground. They had been pulled up from the root. I know it was nothing but the hand of God that protected us. Then I noticed the pecan trees and oak trees that I had assessed and prayed about before the storm, those that towered over our house. Thank God, they were still standing. I know it was God. He spared us. He kept us through the storm.

Storms of Life Will Come

You may never experience firsthand a storm such as a hurricane. But chances are, you will indeed experience the storms of life.

Someone once said, *"You're either in a storm, getting ready to go through a storm, or coming out of a storm."* There's not a person alive who has not or will not encounter the storms of life.

While storms such as hurricanes have certain characteristics, those characteristics are very similar to the storms of life. Hurricanes produce fear. So do the storms of life. Hurricanes produce feelings of hopelessness and helplessness. So do the storms of life. Hurricanes will force you to trust God. So will the storms of life. Prayer is a source of strength during a hurricane. It's also a source of strength during the storms of life.

One of the storms of life I went through came when my granddaughter was born. Every parent and grandparent wants healthy, happy children. As a grandparent waiting on the birth of my granddaughter, it was my prayer that she would be a healthy child. However, shortly before her birth, an ultrasound revealed that there would be challenges.

It was early evening when I arrived at the hospital. My granddaughter was about a week old. Because of the need for more observation and testing, she was not yet allowed to go home. I held her tiny body until she fell asleep, and just minutes after I laid her down, a team of doctors came in. I could tell that some of them were in training. They pulled up my granddaughter's medical records on the computer and examined what looked like x-rays and scans. The doctor who was in charge asked me if I had any questions. I had lots of them. Before they left, one of the doctors stood looking at my granddaughter. I asked him, "Do you think she will ever walk?" He said to me, "No, not without aids."

It was six years ago when the doctor told me my granddaughter would not walk without help. I wish he could have been at her kindergarten dance recital to see her not only walking without her walker, which she started using when she was a toddler, but also dancing, skipping and jumping. As I watched her onstage, my eyes all teary, all I could say was, "Thank you God!" Even today, when my granddaughter goes to visit her doctors, they have a difficult time believing she can put down her walker and walk without it. One doctor even said, "I don't believe her x-rays. They can't be correct. If they were correct, she wouldn't be able to walk at all."

Our family has always been a praying family, and we have a lot of praying friends and relatives. I believe prayer changed the outcome of this storm and gave it a new direction. We trusted in God, and He gave us the desires of our heart. *"Delight yourself also in the Lord, and He shall give you the desires of your heart. Commit your way to the Lord. Trust also in Him, and He shall bring it to pass"* (Psalm 37:4-5).

Storms Serve a Purpose

Storms of life come for different reasons. A storm can be God's way of drawing you closer to Him. It's common when things are going well to live as though you don't really need the Lord. However, God can send a storm into your life that will shake you and make you realize, the only place you can turn is toward Him.

A storm can be God's way of letting you know you need to reprioritize. When something challenging comes into your life, it can help you see that many of the things you thought were important are not so important after all. Being stricken with a life-threatening illness can help you recognize that certain things you thought were important aren't as important as you thought. The office you spend hours and hours working at because you think things will fall apart if you aren't there, you'll realize, it's not that important at all. Even if things do fall apart, in light of your challenge, it's really not that important. In your storms, the lesson God may be trying to teach you is, your relationship with Him should be your top priority.

In the storms of life you will find the opportunity to mature and grow as a person. Challenges refine and fine-tune you. You're pruned and shaped in your challenges. *"Every branch in Me that does not bear fruit He takes away; and every branch that bears fruit He prunes, that it may bear more fruit"* (John 15:2). You may go into a challenge an immature child, but with the proper pruning, you come out a mature Christian.

In any of life's challenges, there will always be practical ways to handle the situation. Determine ways to make changes and take actions that could lessen the stress of your challenge. Always deal with the issue at hand. If you don't, you could find yourself in the same storm over and over again. For example, if you constantly find yourself dealing with challenges that are health-related, it could be the case that you need to take action that could lead to better health, such as focusing on changing your eating habits and getting into an exercise routine. If your challenges seem to always be relationship challenges, you may need to go through a period of self-examination to determine if the problem lies within you. Whatever your challenge, the heart of it needs to be addressed.

Change Your Perception of the Storm

Sometimes the lenses you see life through need to be changed. Change the way you see the situation. The way you see things is the source of the way you react to things. Stop thinking of a situation as something bad or negative. Instead, see it as something God is sending into your life to make you stronger, better. Recognize that no matter what comes into your life, it's something for your good. No matter what it is, it's something God is sending your way to teach you a lesson, to show you something you need to see, to add something of value to your life. Look at life's challenges as opportunities; opportunities to learn, to grow, to prepare you to be able to help someone else who may be getting ready to go through the same storm you're going through.

Surrender to the Storm

Surrendering to the storms in your life doesn't necessarily mean accepting and settling for a certain negative outcome. You can totally surrender and still take action to make necessary changes. In fact, it's not the challenge itself you're surrendering to. You're surrendering to the idea that the situation is real, it happened, and it is what it is. You hold no resistance toward it. The faster you can surrender to the idea that your situation is real and has to be dealt with, the faster you can cut off negative emotions. For example, it's ten o'clock at night and you remember something you were supposed to pick up from the store earlier in the day. It's something you need. You get in your car and head to the store. On your way, you hear a noise. Your car feels a little shaky. You pull over to the side of the road, get out of the car and find out you have a flat tire. A wave of frustration comes over you. You get back into the car and reach for your cell phone. It's not there. You realize you forgot your cell phone.

In an unfortunate situation such as this, you can do one of two things. You can totally resist the situation and allow negative emotions to take over. Or, you can surrender to the situation. Surrendering means you say to yourself, "Okay, I have a flat tire and I forgot my cell phone. I'm not going to panic. I'll start by saying a prayer." Surrendering will keep you from going into panic mode and losing all control of your emotions. It's a real situation. It is what it is, and panicking and losing control is not what is needed.

Hold on to Your Identity in the Storm

When the storms of life come, say to yourself, "I am not my storm." One of the mistakes you can make when experiencing a storm is, you take on the identity of the storm. You can get so lost in negative emotions until you actually think you are the storm. You blame yourself for it. You beat yourself up over it. You wear it on your face and others see it. Then they start to identify you with your storm. They look at you and say, "That's the lady who lost her job." "That's the lady whose husband left her." "That's the lady whose teenage daughter got pregnant." "That's the lady whose husband has cancer." You are not your storm! *"Strength and honor are her clothing. She shall rejoice in time to come"* (Proverbs 31:25). That's really how people should identify you when you're going through life's storms. Instead of wearing your storm, wear strength and honor. This should be your clothing.

When life's challenges come, recognize them for what they are. Ask the question, "Lord, what do you want me to learn in my challenge?" The Bible teaches us to, *"count it all joy when we fall into various trials"* (James 1:2). If you're a child of God, you understand that *"all things work together for good to those who love God, to those who are the called according to His purpose"* (Romans 8:28).

Learn to cast *"all your care upon Him, for He cares for you"* (I Peter 5:7). Spend time in prayer, making your requests known to God. He's your Father, and He loves you. He's there for you in the storms of life. He knows your hurts. He feels your pain. Thank Him. Praise Him. Realize that the storms you experience are part of His plan for your life.

FOR DISCUSSION

1. Have you ever experienced the wrath of a hurricane, tornado or some other natural disaster? Take turns sharing the details of your experience. What were your most frightening moments?

2. Just as natural disasters happen in our lives, we also experience the storms of life, such as a serious illness, the loss of a loved one, losing a house, or losing a job. Many times these are life-changing events. Recall a time in your life when you were hit by a devastating personal storm. How did this change your life? The storms in our lives not only affect us, but others also. How did your storm affect your family and friends? Share some of the tools and principles you used to make it through a storm such as this. Include practical examples such as support systems, as well as spiritual examples, including favorite Scriptures.

3. It's always good when you receive a storm warning that lets you know a storm is coming. It's even better when the storm is over and you find out it wasn't as bad as predicted. Have you ever been anxiously waiting on a test result, only to get the results and find out there was nothing to be alarmed about? Share this experience. During your time of waiting on the results, how did you manage, practically and spiritually? What advice would you give to someone who is waiting on test results and expecting the worse?

4. Sometimes God tries to get our attention. He might call us to do a work. We might simply ignore him, or do everything except what He called us to do. Then we find ourselves in a storm. Read Jonah 1. What was the purpose of the storm God sent to the ship? What lessons did you learn from Jonah 1?

5. Name other individuals in the Bible who went through personal storms? Share some of their stories. Give Scriptures.

6. Some of the storms we experience in life can be avoided if we take proper measures and precautions. Discuss some of them and talk about ways to avoid them. See page 127.

7. There's nothing like a sense of peace when you're in the midst of a storm. Have you ever been in a storm but felt an unusual sense of peace? Share your experience. Find Scriptures on peace and share them.

8. Sometimes the personal storms that come into our lives can make us or break us. What does this mean?

9. Read Matthew 14:22-33. Discuss the details of this story and how it can encourage us when we are going through a storm. What would you say is the strongest point of this story?

10. Sometimes the lenses you see life through need to be changed. Change the way you see the situation. Discuss the meaning of this statement from page 127.

Chapter 13

Be a Virtuous Woman

"The Baptism"

"Charm is deceitful and beauty is passing,
but a woman who fears the Lord,
she shall be praised" (Proverbs 31:30).

It was a few weeks after Vacation Bible School when I decided to go to my mother and ask if I could be baptized. I was only eight years old, so I wasn't sure what her response would be. Our family was a church-going family, that is, except my dad. While he stayed home, my mother gathered all seven of us up on Sunday mornings and off to church we went. I don't remember ever missing a Sunday. And years later, after we were all grown and out of the house, my dad started going.

I had several reasons I wanted to be baptized. First of all, I had heard from the preacher the story of Jesus dying on the cross for our sins, and I believed it. I had learned that if you believed this story and was baptized, after your baptism, your sins were washed away and you were forgiven for everything you'd ever done wrong. Well, considering what my grandmother told me about something I'd been doing, I figured I needed to be baptized.

At the time, I was a huge Jackson Five fan. I loved to watch Michael Jackson and his brothers dance and perform on television.

However, one day, my grandmother told me I was committing a sin by watching the Jackson Five because of all the dancing they did. She said it was a sin to dance. Well, I had learned enough in church to know that I didn't want to miss heaven and go to that place called hell. So, when I began to struggle with the issue of dancing and watching the Jackson Five on television, I thought I'd better do the right thing; be baptized and have all of my sins washed away.

After my mother was convinced that I was mature enough and understood well enough what I was doing, she and the minister agreed to allow the baptism to take place. I wore a white dress with short sleeves as I walked up the aisle and gave the minister my hand. As I stood there next to him, he asked me to state to the audience why I wanted to be baptized. Since I was so young, I guess he wanted to make sure they knew I had been counseled and understood what I was doing. After being baptized, I went home feeling like a new person.

Well, needless to say, when the newness of my baptism wore off, I learned that being baptized didn't stop me from committing sins, not even the one my grandmother labeled as sin; dancing. But, I thank God because I have since learned that by His grace and by the power of His Holy Spirit, as long as I'm striving to live the life of a virtuous woman, when I sin, the blood of Christ cleanses me. *"But if we walk in the light as He is in the light, we have fellowship with one another, and the blood of Jesus Christ His Son cleanses us from all sin"* (I John 1:7).

The Woman of Virtue

A virtuous woman is a woman whose life is guided by moral and ethical principles. She's a woman of integrity who conforms to a standard of righteousness. She's strong, courageous and confident. She's influential, a woman of honor. *"Strength and honor are her clothing. She shall rejoice in time to come"* (Proverbs 31:25).

Being a woman of virtue should be the goal of every woman, and while I was fortunate to come to know the Lord at a young age, my journey toward becoming a virtuous woman has been a long, challenging one. If you grew up around the same time I grew up, you were probably lacking in teachings on what it meant to be a virtuous woman. In fact, I've often wondered whether or not it would have made a difference in my life had someone shared with me what it meant to be a girl of virtue. Would I have avoided many of the mistakes I made? I wonder if it would have made a difference if someone had said to me, "Remain pure and innocent. Hold on to your virginity. God meant it for marriage."

When I was a young girl, teachings from my parents and grandparents were very vague, and sometimes had no real meaning. Can you remember a time in your young life when somebody sat you down and had a conversation about remaining a virgin and why it was important? I heard things like, "Keep your dress down!" "Leave those boys alone!" As a young girl, that was pretty much the extent of my teachings on becoming a virtuous woman.

When I look back on my childhood and the experiences I've had, I certainly can't blame my parents for the mistakes and bad choices I've made. Where I am is where I'm supposed to be, and the experiences I've had all add up to make me who I am. My parents and grandparents did the best they could to rear us, train us and prepare us for a successful journey through life.

The Single Woman of Virtue

Becoming a virtuous woman is not something that happens overnight. It's a process that takes time. Virtue comes with spiritual growth and personal development. It comes with studying the Word of God, praying and being open and honest. A woman desiring virtue must be willing to admit her shortcomings, submit to the will of

God and admit her need for God's Holy Spirit. Becoming a virtuous woman comes with sitting at the feet of other virtuous women who can share wisdom and honesty about their own journey toward virtue. *"The older women likewise, that they be reverent in behavior, not slanderers, not given to much wine, teachers of good things—that they admonish the young women to love their husbands, to love their children, to be discreet, chaste, homemakers, good, obedient to their own husbands, that the word of God may not be blasphemed"* (Titus 2:3-5). Older women have a story to share. They've already been down many of the roads you're trying to travel. They can teach you and share the challenges they've endured, helping you avoid the same mistakes they made.

If you think you have to be married to be a virtuous woman, you're wrong. Single women, too, must strive to be virtuous women. I was recently speaking to a small group of women, most of them single. We made a list of challenges single women are facing in this day and time. The list included things like difficulty finding a godly prospect for a husband, difficulty abstaining from sexual relationships, entering into intimate relationships with men for the sake of having help paying the bills, overcoming a criminal background, being in abusive relationships and lack of spiritual focus. The issue we seemed to spend the most time on was the issue of finding a godly prospect for a husband.

Some single women want so badly to be in a relationship that they settle for a man, any man. If he doesn't meet godly standards, they go into the relationship with the attitude, "I'll change him." Or, "We'll make it work." It's one of the biggest mistakes single women make.

If you're a single woman, focus on spiritual things, on the Lord and His will for your life. *"There is a difference between a wife and a virgin. The unmarried woman cares about the things of the Lord, that she may be holy both in body and in spirit. But she who is married cares about the things of the world—how she may please her husband"* (1 Corinthians 7:34). There are many single women who think it's God's will that they find a husband and get married. This is their life's mission, and it brings a lot of stress into their lives. It's not necessarily the case that God wants you in a marriage relationship. The first place God wants you is in a relationship with Him. In fact, it could be the case that He knows you can work more effectively in His kingdom as a single woman. Perhaps He knows that a husband might change your spiritual DNA.

If you're a single mother, instead of focusing on what your life would be like as a married woman, focus on the Lord and His will for your life. He's the best friend you can have. Then, focus on raising your children, teaching your daughters what it means to be a girl of virtue. Teach them the importance of keeping their virginity, knowing their value and worth and how to select godly friends. Teach them to develop their own relationship with God by studying the Bible, praying and being obedient. Be a godly example to them. Let them see you living as a virtuous woman lives. Be careful of who you allow to have access to your children. Not everyone should be allowed to baby—sit your children or pick them up from school. Know their friends and the parents of their friends.

Get into God. The more you get into Him, the more He'll get into you. Wrap yourself in His presence and in the things that are important to Him.

The Married Woman of Virtue

Picture yourself standing in front of a person with your back toward them, and they tell you to close your eyes and fall back into their arms so they can catch you. Can you think of people in your life you would trust to catch you when you fall? No doubt, this would have to be somebody you really trust. That's certainly the case for me. It would have to be someone I know has my best interest at heart;

someone who will be strong enough to keep me from falling. The only person I think I would trust to catch me is my husband!

When you trust someone, you know that person has your safety and security in mind. They're concerned about your physical as well as your emotional wellbeing. If you're a wife, you know the importance of trust. You expect to be able to trust your husband, and he expects you to be trustworthy. *"The heart of her husband safely trusts her; so he will have no lack of gain. She does him good and not evil all the days of her life"* (Proverbs 31:11-12). Trust is the foundation of any healthy relationship.

One of the greatest barriers to trust in the marriage relationship is when one or the other spouse allows infidelity to enter the relationship. To engage in infidelity is to engage in an inappropriate relationship with someone who's not your spouse. There was a time when men were the ones more likely to cheat and engage in infidelity. But today, infidelity on the part of the woman has increased. Many women are engaging in such. As the years have brought more women into the workforce, women have become more independent, and this seems to have a connection with infidelity. If you are a career woman working a fulltime job, you more than likely spend more waking hours at work with other men than you do at home. Developing an intimate relationship with a co-worker is something that can happen, and it does happen. Another factor is the Internet, which has made it easier for women to meet, chat with and develop relationships with other men. These types of cyberspace meetings can not only lead to physical relationships, but can also lead to emotional affairs.

An emotional affair is a relationship with another man where there is no inappropriate physical contact. He simply provides you with emotional support. Perhaps he compliments you and comforts you. This affair can be just as destructive as an affair of a physical nature. You long to talk to this man. You engage in long telephone conversations with him, whether it's while you're at work, or even at home. Perhaps he has a good listening ear. He fills a void and provides you with a level of emotional support you feel is missing from your life.

This type of unhealthy relationship can do much destruction in your marriage. If you are in an emotional affair, know that just because there is no physical contact, this does not mean there's nothing wrong with what you are doing. If you think there's nothing wrong with it, tell your husband about the relationship and ask his opinion. If you're in a relationship you cannot share with your husband, you should end that relationship.

She Dresses in Modest Apparel

"And do not be conformed to this world, but be transformed by the renewing of your mind, that you may prove what is that good and acceptable and perfect will of God" (Romans 12:2). The world has a powerful, magnetic force that can easily attract us and steal our focus if we don't keep ourselves clothed in *"the whole armor of God"* (Ephesians 6:11). One of the ways we can find ourselves conforming to the world's standards is when we conform to the dress code society has established for women. Society has succeeded on many fronts in convincing women that anything goes when it comes to the way a woman dresses. If we're not careful, we can find ourselves dressing in attire that's not appropriate for women of God.

Have you ever put on an outfit, looked in the mirror and got an uncomfortable feeling about the image in the mirror? Perhaps you put on a pair of jeans and when you looked at yourself in the mirror, the fit was a bit tight, a little too revealing. Or, if it was a skirt or dress, perhaps the hemline was a little too high. It was above your knees.

There was a time when a woman would put on a dress, look in the mirror, and if the dress seemed too revealing, she'd immediately feel a sense of shame or discomfort at the thought of actually wearing the garment. But today, that's not always the case. It's not uncommon to see, even in the church, women dressed in attire that's simply not appropriate for those who profess to be women of God. There are several things women can do to contribute to a more modest style of dressing.

A while ago, I was in the mall shopping with my mother. I found a red dress I wanted to try on. After finding the size I needed, I went into the dressing room and tried it on. It was a fitted dress, so I got a size larger because I didn't want the tight fit around my waist and hips. Because it was a larger size, it was a little too loose under the arms. The dress only had a short cap sleeve and because it was loose, it exposed a little too much around the underarm. My actual size probably would have been a better fit in the underarm area, but tighter than I liked in the waist and hips. My only option was to buy a jacket to wear with it. After much contemplation, I decided against the purchase.

I exited the dressing room and hung the dress on the rack right outside the dressing room. As I left the room, a young woman was on her way in. She saw the red dress I had just hung on the rack. She stopped to look at it, took it off the rack and carried it into the dressing room along with the other garments she was going to try on. The lady, who seemed to be at least a couple of sizes larger than the size I wore, later came out of the dressing room, went to the counter, and among the items she paid for was the red dress. It's difficult for me to believe she could comfortably fit the dress. I could be wrong, but I doubt it. Buying sizes too small is a common purchase decision a lot of women consciously make.

If you're concerned about making sure you purchase clothing that fits well, is comfortable, modest, yet attractive, perhaps some dressing room tips will help as you shop. If you're in the dressing room trying on a dress, after you get it on, pay attention to the fit. A dress is too tight if you have to struggle to zip it. It's also too tight if it's difficult for you to breathe once you get it on. What does it look like in the mirror? If you're in a smaller dressing room, you may have to walk outside the dressing room where there is usually a much larger, three-way mirror that will show you everything you need to see. Stand in front of the mirror. Look at the breast area of the dress. If you see cleavage, the dress is not appropriate. Usually, when you put on an outfit that shows a little cleavage, by the time you get where you're going, the dress has made its own adjustments and is exposing even more of your breasts. Now, turn just enough to see your rear. If you can see panty lines, this is another indicator that a dress, skirt or slacks may be too tight.

Perhaps you've grown and matured to the point that you're conscious and selective of what you wear to church. However, it's not uncommon to see you in a public place dressed in attire that's not appropriate. No matter where you're going, use wisdom and show spiritual maturity in determining what's appropriate to wear. You may not show cleavage or wear a dress or outfit that's too revealing to church, but may have no problem going to the mall wearing a blouse that exposes too much, or wearing some other outfit that attracts attention because it leaves nothing to the imagination. There are some things that are not appropriate for a woman of God, no matter where she's going.

You may ask, "Why does it matter what I wear?" The Bible sets the standard for the way a woman dresses. God cares about your appearance. "*In like manner also, that the women adorn themselves in modest apparel, with propriety and moderation, not with braided hair or gold or pearls or costly clothing, but, which is proper for women professing godliness, with good works*" (I Timothy 2:9-10).

Spiritual growth is really the key to conquering and overcoming this issue. As a woman grows and matures in her relationship with God, her level of commitment and obedience to Him grows. When you walk in obedience to the Lord, it's not a chore to live holy and godly. It's not a chore to dress in modest apparel. You do it because you love God, you love His Word and you're striving to live the life of a virtuous woman. As you grow and mature in the Lord and in His Word, changes happen on the inside, and when the inside changes, the outside will follow.

FOR DISCUSSION

1. What are some characteristics of a virtuous woman? Share Scriptures.
2. Who were some of the virtuous women in the Bible? Share Scriptures.
3. What are some of a virtuous single woman's greatest challenges? Share ways to overcome these challenges.
4. What are some of a virtuous married woman's greatest challenges? Share ways to overcome these challenges.
5. Think back on your childhood. Can you recall a conversation with your mother, grandmother, aunt, or some other close relative about what it meant to be chaste? What are the consequences of young girls finding out about matters of intimacy from their friends and acquaintances?
6. It seems that many of our teen and pre-teen girls are struggling with issues that many of us weren't exposed to until we were much older than they are; having intimate physical relationships as early as junior high, engaging in lesbian relationships, abusive dating relationships and other unfortunate circumstances. As a society, and as a church, where did we go wrong? How can we help our young girls become the virtuous women God wants them to be?
7. Read 1 Timothy 2:9. There will always be conversations about what's modest and what's not. However, there are some basic rules of dressing that can be followed to keep us in the safety zone when it comes to what we wear. What are some of those rules?
8. Suppose a sister who is a new babe in Christ regularly comes to church provocatively dressed. Should this situation be addressed? Who are those who should address it and why? Give supporting Scripture(s).

9. It's important that seasoned sisters be an example in how to dress for those who are not as seasoned. Sometimes seeing a sermon is even more powerful than hearing one. Share your thoughts on these statements.

10. Becoming a Christian doesn't mean we have a free ticket to heaven. In our day and age, temptations are all around us and we can find ourselves giving in. Share keys to staying saved.

Chapter 14

Take Off the Mask

"Afternoon of Play"

*"Put on the whole armor of God,
that you may be able to stand against the
wiles of the devil" (Ephesians 6:11).*

It was a couple of weeks before an upcoming speaking engagement. I like to use visuals, so I'd purchased a half mask with a handle that allowed me to hold it over my face. The silver metallic mask was really pretty. It was trimmed in silver beads, lace and ribbons. Unfortunately, I had a difficult time finding it and ended up having to pay way more than I'd planned to spend. I splurged on it because I knew it would be perfect for my speech, which was entitled, "Take Off the Mask."

It was Thursday, and my granddaughter was with me for the day. She was out of school with an ear infection. But to see her running around playing with her grocery cart, paper dolls and other toys, you would never have known she was in the doctor's office with a terrible earache just a few hours prior.

As my granddaughter played around in my living room, it didn't take her long to spot the shiny, glittering mask lying on the coffee table, and of course she was fascinated with it. It seemed to fit right in with the other toys she was playing with. She held the expensive mask up to her face as she wheeled her grocery cart through the house. She wanted me to guess who was behind the mask.

This was early afternoon. When it was getting close to time for my husband to get home, Cyniah took her mask and got underneath the table. When I noticed her under the table, I asked, "Little Missy, why are you under the table?" She said, "I'm going to hide from Big Daddy so when he comes into the house, I'll come out with my mask on and he won't know who I am." I thought to myself, "Maybe I'll do the same thing and he won't know who I am and won't ask me why I didn't cook today."

After getting tired of hiding under the table and finally realizing that Big Daddy might be a little late coming home, Cyniah decided to come out from hiding, get her grocery cart and make a few more rounds through the house. As I watched her stroll with her grocery cart in one hand and the mask covering her face in the other, she became the embodiment of what I would talk about in my speech; women who wear masks that cover their real identity.

Which Mask Are You Wearing

There are many masks to choose from. There's the mask that says, "I'm alright. I've got it all together. Things are just great in my world." There's the mask that says, "I've got low self-esteem." There's another mask that says, "I'm so busy." There's one that says, "I'm so worried." If you wear masks, be careful. You can wear a mask for so long until you really think the face you're wearing is you, when actually, the real you is hiding behind the mask. You can wear your mask for so long until you totally lose touch with the real you. In this fast-paced, busy world we live in, it is indeed possible to lose touch with yourself, to lose touch with the real you.

How would you answer the question, "Who are you?" You would probably say, "I'm a mother." "I'm a wife." "I'm a teacher." "I'm a lawyer." "I'm an entertainer." "I'm a writer." You may say any one of these, or something else. When you answer the question with answers such as this, you haven't answered who you are. You've basically described what you do in your everyday life. What you do is not who you are. But you've done those things for so long until you think you are what you do. You are totally lost in what you do. The real you is hidden, totally obscured, covered by a mask. Will the real you please stand up!

The Bible says Jesus entered a certain village, and a woman named Martha invited Him to her home. Martha had a sister named Mary, and while Jesus visited, Mary sat at His feet and listened to Him. But Martha, the Bible says, was busy serving. Actually, the Bible says she was *"distracted with much serving"* (Luke 10:40). It was obvious Martha had something on her mind that day. Perhaps she was frustrated. This was apparent in her expression to Jesus when she said, *"Lord, do You not care that my sister has left me to serve alone? Therefore tell her to help me"* (Luke 10:40). This sounds like someone who's frustrated. Have you ever been frustrated over a larger issue, but instead of addressing the larger issue, you allow yourself to be "set off" by smaller, petty issues? Jesus responded to Martha. *"And Jesus answered and said to her, „ Martha, Martha, you are worried and troubled about many things. But one thing is needed, and Mary has chosen that good part, which will not be taken away from her"'* (Luke 10:41-42).

It's possible to wear more than one mask. It seems that Martha wore the mask called "I'm so worried." As well, she covered this mask with one called "I'm so busy."

The "I'm So Busy" Mask

Perhaps you're wearing the "I'm so busy" mask. This is by far the most popular mask women wear. The woman who wears this mask is always on the move, always on the go. She's dropping off someone here, picking up someone there. She volunteers for everything. She volunteers to bake cupcakes for her child's homeroom holiday party. She volunteers to head up the fundraisers for the school. She volunteers to take the lead in planning the school fall festival. She volunteers to be a helper in the classroom. She volunteers to make the costumes for the school holiday program. She volunteers for just about everything. At church, she's on several different ministries. She teaches Sunday school. She does kitchen duty. She's on the visitation ministry, the married couples ministry, the new members ministry. You name it; she does it. And when she's not volunteering to do something, she's agreeing to do something someone has asked her to do. She never says "no." She agrees to baby-sit her friend's kids for the weekend. She agrees to pick up her neighbor from work until her car gets repaired. And every weekend her children have an agenda that she has to follow. Her eighteen year old has to go to the mall. Her fifteen year old has to meet at the church for a youth function. Her eight year old has baseball practice. This woman has worn the "I'm so busy" mask for so long, until she thinks it's who she really is.

Women who wear this mask can't function outside of a busy schedule. Does this describe you? During those rare occasions when you have a window where you have a little down time, you don't know what to do with it. You don't know how to sit and just be alone with yourself. You get anxious and uncomfortable and before you know it, you're engaged in some meaningless task that's just something to fill your time. Remember Martha, who was *distracted with much serving?*" I wonder if serving was her way of staying busy so she wouldn't have to face those things that were really troubling her? Why do you wear the "I'm so busy" mask? Why are you hiding the real person behind the mask?

How do you find the person underneath the mask? How do you take off the "I'm so busy" mask? First of all, know that God has built some mechanisms into your body that will cause it to shut down if you don't take off the "I'm so busy" mask. Surely you don't have time for sickness and hospital stays. But that's what could happen if you don't slow down. When you are always on the go, it leaves little time for eating right, exercising and taking care of your body. You're putting an unnatural amount of stress on your body and this could lead to a weakened immune system, which could leave you susceptible to different types of illnesses. Not only does your physical body suffer, so does your spiritual life. Your busy lifestyle leaves little time for prayer and studying God's Word, spending time in His presence.

Secondly, start examining each task you set out to do and challenge the task. Don't do it if it's not something essential. And, don't feel guilty when you say "no." It's all right to say "no" as long as you know you're saying it out of a genuine heart, and you know accepting a task would not result in a higher good. Saying "no" will free up some of your time and allow you to begin scheduling quiet time. Quiet moments will help you slowly start to peel off the "I'm so busy mask." It may be uncomfortable at first, but as you begin enjoying your time alone, it will become more comfortable.

Finally, you need to find out why you need the mask. Why are you uncomfortable when you don't have something to do? Is there something about yourself personally that you're uncomfortable with, something that makes you not want to be alone with yourself? Is there something about your life you are not satisfied with but don't know how to change? You need to find the heart of the issue. There's nothing wrong with having a productive daily schedule. However, when you use your busy lifestyle as a cover-up, it's like sweeping yourself under a rug.

The "I'm So Worried" Mask

Another mask that's likely familiar is the "I'm so worried mask." The Bible clearly teaches against being filled with worry. *"Be anxious for nothing, but in everything by prayer and supplication, with thanksgiving, let your requests be made known to God; and the peace of God, which surpasses all understanding, will guard your hearts and minds through Christ Jesus"* (Philippians 4:6-7).

In our day and time, it's a challenge to keep from becoming overwhelmed by stress and worry. Many individuals have an entire list of worries they deal with from day to day. What's your worry? Are you worrying because of a recent medical diagnosis? This can certainly bring on stress. Are you worrying because of a recent layoff from your job? Layoffs seem to be a common occurrence in our day and time, leaving individuals with anxiety and uncertainty. There are all kinds of worries. You may be worrying about a wayward child, a pregnant teen, or a child behind bars. These can certainly bring on stress and worry. Losing a loved one can bring on stress and worry. Marital problems can bring on stress and worry. These are just a few of the situations that will invite worry into your life.

Worrying is a normal reaction when something happens that threatens to bring unwanted or negative changes into your life. However, as a child of God, worrying is not something that should linger in your spirit and become a part of your normal state of mind. A child of God should never be seen with the "I'm so worried" mask on. Instead of putting on this mask, recognize your challenge for what it is. *"Count it all joy when you fall into various trials"* (James 1:2). Also, don't be afraid to open up and share your worries with godly people, those who can share with you and encourage you in your efforts to take off the "I'm so worried" mask. People are God's vessels. He works through people. Opening up and sharing with others opens the door to those people God has prepared to minister to you.

Taking Off the Mask

It's time to strip away the masks and start dealing with the challenges and issues in our lives. It's time to stop being out of touch with our bodies and unfamiliar with what's going on inside of us. Our lives are so busy and noisy until we can't even hear ourselves hurting.

Taking off the mask doesn't mean that underneath the masks we wear, there's a sinless, perfect individual. That's not the case. Christ is the only perfect One, and as Christians, we are to clothe ourselves in His perfect righteousness. The Bible teaches, "*I have been crucified with Christ; it is no longer I who live, but Christ lives in me; and the life which I now live in the flesh I live by faith in the Son of God, who loved me and gave Himself for me*" (Galatians 2:20). "*For you died, and your life is hidden with Christ in God*" (Colossians 3:3).

As children of God, our lives are hidden in Christ, and He calls us to glorify Him in everything. Everything we do should be to His glory and reflect His righteousness. "*Therefore, whether you eat or drink, or whatever you do, do all to the glory of God*" (1 Corinthians 10:31).

If something as simple and common as eating and drinking is to be done to the glory of God, surely He requires you to reflect His glory in the way you manage your life. The Bible teaches, "*Present your bodies a living sacrifice, holy, acceptable to God, which is your reasonable service*" (Romans 12:1).

Use wisdom in managing your life. Mary, the sister of Martha, knew when to say "no." She could have been busying herself in the kitchen with Martha. But instead, she chose "*that good part*" (Luke 10:42). She chose to sit at the feet of Jesus. When your life is hidden in Christ, you know and accept those things that are good for you, and reject those things that do not promote a higher good for your life.

FOR DISCUSSION

1. A mask is something a woman might put on when she doesn't want to reveal her true identity; her true feelings and emotions to others. What are some reasons we sometimes go to that place where we simply don't want to show what's real?

2. What are some of the masks we wear?

3. Is wearing a mask always a negative? When is wearing a mask a positive? What is a major problem with wearing a mask too long? (See page 144)

4. When you take off the "I've got it all together" mask, you might be allowing a sister in pain to see that she's not alone. The two of you are going through the same challenge. Discuss this idea.

5. It's important to be able to just be yourself and not have to wear a mask. However, a lack of trust can be a major reason for wearing a mask. As sisters, what can we do to earn trust from one another?

6. Read Luke 10:38-42. Martha was wearing a mask. In fact, she could have possibly been wearing more than one. Which masks did Martha seem to be wearing?

7. Sometimes we can put on a mask but even with the mask on, because our emotions and energy are so strong and powerful, it's difficult to hide the real person. Discuss this idea.

8. How do we know Jesus saw through the masks Martha wore? Give Scripture(s).

9. Were there any indications that Mary might have had on a mask? Give reasons for your answer.

10. What are the keys to putting away the masks we wear and just being ourselves? Give Scriptures such as Romans 12:2.

Chapter 15

Take Responsibility

"The Candy Dish"

"So then each of us shall give account of himself to God" (Romans 14:12).

I was just a child, maybe eight years old or so, when my mother purchased that cute little porcelain candy dish. It had soft splendid colors that blended together and seemed to change colors with every movement. I was with my mom when she found the perfect place for the candy dish. She carefully positioned it on the table that sat at the end of the sofa. Then she made it clear to me that I was not to touch it.

My mother was familiar with my habits and knew I would find the candy dish fascinating and want to explore its beauty with my little fingers. That's why she made it a point to tell me not to touch it. Well, one day as I sat in the room all alone gazing at the beautiful little dish, a battle started warring inside of me. I said to myself, "I sure want to touch it. But, what if I touch it and break it?" Then I thought, "Oh, I won't break it. I'll just pick it up and put it right back down and no one will ever know." This little war went on for quite a while. Finally, I just couldn't resist. I got up and went over to the candy dish. I picked it up and pulled it toward me. As I began to explore it, the beautiful piece of porcelain slipped right out of my little hands and onto the floor. The dish was heavier than I calculated, and therefore, it didn't shatter. In fact, it broke into three pieces. In my fear, devastation and humiliation, I stooped to pick up the broken pieces. I had to think fast.

I took the pieces and cleverly fitted them back together like I had learned to piece together a puzzle. The pieces fit together perfectly. The candy dish sat on the table as if there was nothing wrong with it. I backed away and left the room.

I guess I thought that would be the end of it. However, for the next few days, I was tormented. Once again, a war was going on. Guilt was consuming me. I knew what I had done was wrong and I had to make it right. But I was only a child. I had never had to go to anyone and ask for forgiveness, especially not my mom. Finally, I couldn't take the weight of the guilt any longer. I knew I had disobeyed my mother and I had to go to her and tell her what I had done.

Oh how I remember that day, the day I went to my mom. I remember going to her and looking her in the face, and I remember the look on her face. My mother was very serious when it came to our behavior. She didn't mind disciplining us when we got out of line. I was the fifth child of seven, and she treated us all the same when it came to correcting our behavior. So choosing to tell her what I had done was no small decision. As I looked into her face, I said to her, "Mama, you know the candy dish?" "Yes," she replied. After a bit of hesitation, I responded, "I broke it." It was a painful experience having to say those words to my mom. I could see her face turn into a frown, and then slowly the frown went away. My mother responded by saying, "I already knew."

That experience was many years ago, and the lesson I learned as a child would shape the world in which I live even now. After the confession to my mother, I felt relieved, released and free. The lesson from that day was that true empowerment comes from being honest and accepting responsibility for your actions. After that experience, life continued to happen and it didn't take long for me to learn that I wasn't as perfect as I wanted to be. And even as I went on to experience life in the many mistakes I've made and in the many flaws and imperfections I've found in myself, I still thank God for giving me that one particular experience that taught me at a very young age the value of taking responsibility.

Learning Responsibility

You've heard the saying, "The devil made me do it!" Well, that's the attitude many in society have and it basically means, "I'm not responsible." My husband and I have an adult son, and I can't count the number of times we've said, "Son, you need to become more responsible."

Perhaps you're a parent with a plan for your child's future. However, things aren't working out the way you planned. Instead of embracing adulthood by leaving the comfort of your home to find his or her own productive place in society, your young adult still lives with you. Or perhaps they went off to college, but after college because of a lack of job opportunities, they had no choice but to move back home. Society has a name for children who move back home to live with their parents. They're called "boomerang kids." And while there are a number of reasons children might find themselves back in the "nest," including economic reasons, there's still way too many young adults living with parents simply because they never learned the value of responsible behavior. A failure on your part to teach your child responsibility could very well be the reason they are still enjoying the comfort of your home, and until responsible behavior is learned, you may never know the experience of being an "empty nester."

Responsible behavior is learned, and it's learned at an early age. If you're a responsible person, somewhere along life's journey, you learned this behavior. On the other hand, if you're struggling and having difficulty becoming the responsible individual you know you need to be, it could be the case that in your past, you lived in an environment where you were not encouraged to be responsible. You were not held accountable, not held to a standard of accountability.

One of the greatest lessons you can learn in life is the fact that no one is responsible for your life but you. This is a biblical principle that unfortunately, many fail to learn. The Bible teaches, *"But let each one examine his own work, and then he will have rejoicing in himself alone, and not in another. For each one shall bear his own load"* (Galatians 6:4-5). You are responsible for every aspect of your life; how you feel, how you think, what you do, the decisions you make and the impact on your life those decisions will have. You are responsible for the direction of your life, for structuring your life with balance and harmony and for nurturing your health and emotional well-being.

When you assume responsibility for your life, you recognize that you are your greatest supporter. You are the star of your own show, and no one should believe in you more than you believe in yourself. Don't depend on others to make you feel good about yourself. You are responsible for making yourself feel good. Don't allow others to determine and dictate the development of your self-esteem and self-confidence. That's your responsibility. If you don't like your life, reinvent it. Every moment has in it the opportunity for change, the opportunity to change the way you live. The challenges of life are sometimes labeled as "lemons." There may be times when life hands you a "lemon." Lemons are tangy and challenging to swallow, and so are some of life's difficulties. If you should receive a "lemon," don't whine and complain about it. Take ownership of it and make "lemonade."

I recently noticed a new lady in my yoga class. At the end of class during our tea session, she introduced herself.

After class ended, I went out into the office area and hung around to wait for my instructor. She and I had planned to talk that day after class, so I took a seat next to her desk and waited. As I sat there, I saw my instructor walking out of the room where tea had been served. She was engaged in a conversation with the new lady who walked beside her. I heard the woman say to my instructor, "I was laid off from my job. That's why I'm here at the morning class." Just as she finished her sentence, she looked at me. She could tell I was listening to their conversation. Before she could say anything to me, I asked, "Did I hear you say you got laid off?" "Yes," she replied. I responded to her, "Just look at this as a new beginning."

This prompted the lady to open up and speak freely about her layoff. She talked about how she had been treated unfairly at work and said she wasn't the one who should have gotten laid off. She blamed her layoff on someone who told the boss something negative about her. As she spoke, she became emotional. I reiterated to her, "Just look at this as a new beginning; something that was supposed to happen."

When life hands you a challenge, be careful how you handle it. The woman in my class is certainly a candidate for getting stuck in a place it's difficult to get out of. She placed the blame for her layoff on someone else, instead of seeing her situation as something she should take control of and turn into something positive. She could very easily get bogged down in bitterness and animosity toward the people she worked with. Negative emotions can turn into negative energy and if you're not careful, this can lead to destructive behavior.

Perhaps you're the person who was laid off, or maybe you're going through some other challenge. It doesn't matter why you're in the situation you're in. Accepting responsibility doesn't mean someone else is not to blame for your situation. It means you are willing to release yourself of the control you allow them to have over your thoughts and actions. It means you stop lamenting and being consumed with what others have done to you. The important thing is to recognize your situation for what it is, accept responsibility for where you are and start planning your strategy for moving forward.

The Blame Game

Do you play the blame game when you begin to endure negative consequences or when things are not going well in your life? To play the blame game is to make everything somebody else's fault. Nothing that ever happens is your fault. It's easier to just blame someone else.

There's usually a pattern with people who play the blame game. If you're the person who plays this game, those you spend the most time with probably recognize the following pattern in you. You never think you're wrong, even when everyone else can see that you're wrong. You have an answer for everything and in your own way, even though you're the only one who can see your point, you stand your ground and won't back down. You live in the past, always bringing up situations that happened in your past. You easily get defensive when confronted. When you believe someone is about to confront you and hold you accountable, you immediately start defending yourself. You believe life is unfair and think you can never get ahead. You feel you're not capable of ever making a positive difference. You have a constant need for someone to pat you on the back and make you feel good. And finally, you constantly make excuses and try to justify yourself when you fail to do what you said you would do. These are characteristics of a person known for playing the blame game.

Know that when you play the blame game, what you're really doing is making an attempt to cover up the real issues and the heart of a challenge. Perhaps you're the woman who lives in the past and blame others for where you are. Your mother and father weren't always there when you were growing up, so maybe you didn't get the love and support you needed. Perhaps you were sexually or emotionally abused when you were a child and suffered all kinds of other injustices. Now you blame your mother for not protecting you and your father for not being there. You believe they're the reason you are where you are. Your self-esteem is low. You feel like there's no hope for you. You feel like you have no choice but to live a miserable life. Others caused your unhappiness. It's your co-worker's fault you got fired. It's you ex-husband's fault you had to get a roommate to help make ends meet.

As long as you allow negative feelings and emotions to consume you, it will be difficult to get to the heart of your challenges. The best way to begin getting to the root of your problems is to stop playing the blame game and make the decision to take full responsibility for your life, even if your unfortunate circumstances are not your fault.

The Cost of Responsibility

To take responsibility is to take ownership, and with ownership comes cost and sacrifice. Responsibility is hardly ever without cost, and many simply don't accept responsibility because of the cost that comes with it. It may not be a monetary cost, but chances are, when you take on responsibility, you will be required to expend some form of investment such as time, energy and effort. And sometimes, these are more difficult to sacrifice than money.

In marriage, being responsible comes with an expensive price tag. You can check just about any research on marriage and divorce statistics and you will find that fifty percent of marriages end in divorce. It's also a fact that many who remain in the marriage relationship engage in extramarital affairs. Staggering statistics such as this is a result of an unwillingness to pay the cost that comes with marriage. When you were single, perhaps you were able to spend your free time doing whatever you chose to do. However, when you said, "I do," that changed. Now that you're married, your free time should be shared with your spouse. Being a responsible marriage partner requires not only a sacrifice of time, but also of space, money, energy and much more.

Perhaps you are a parent. If so, you have a choice of being a responsible parent or an irresponsible parent. Responsible parents make costly sacrifices. Spending quality time with your children is going to cost something. It's going to cost a certain amount of time out of your schedule. Responsible parents make sure their children have what they need for everyday life; food, clothes, shelter and other resources. This requires an expensive monetary sacrifice.

On the other hand, one of the greatest social ills plaguing society today is the issue of irresponsible parents; parents who fail to take on the responsibility of caring for their children. This is not uncommon in single parent homes where you might find a single mother struggling to make ends meet due to a lack of support from the child's father. Many times, the reason support is not provided is due to the monetary cost required on the part of the father who is unwilling to make the costly sacrifice.

There seems to be an epidemic among many in society when it comes to irresponsible behavior. Jails are filled to capacity with many who are there because of irresponsible behavior, an unwillingness to bear the cost of responsibility; instead, opting for robbery, trickery, deception, and manipulation; trying to get something for nothing. According to the U.S. Bureau of Justice Statistics, at the end of the year 2009, 7,225,800 people were on probation, in jail or prison, or on parole—one in 32 adults, or about 3.1 percent of U.S. adult residents.

The bottom line is, with responsibility comes cost, and many fail to accept responsibility because of the cost that comes with it.

Examining Yourself

No doubt, you know someone or have known someone who just can't seem to be able to get his or her life together. They simply stumble through life. When they get on their feet, before long, they've fallen down again. Things go well for a while. Then the cycle of ups and downs start all over. This may even describe your life. If you're the person struggling to find a place of peace, fulfillment and contentment in life, one of the first things you can do is find someone to talk to, someone with whom you can share your innermost feelings.

It helps to have someone you can be accountable to, someone who will hold you to a higher standard in your every day walk. Opening up and sharing promotes good mental and emotional health as you share your life, talk about where you are in life and where you want to be. A wise, godly person can help you see a clearer vision for your future and help you see the benefits of taking responsibility for your life. They can teach and mentor you.

Then start examining yourself and your life and find where improvements need to be made. While a godly friend can counsel you and help you get on the right track, they can't live your life for you. It's up to you to start doing things differently. If you keep doing the same old things, you'll get the same old results. If you are not progressing in life, it's not always someone else's fault. It could be the case that you haven't been engaging in things that lead to progress. If you're not maturing in your spiritual walk, perhaps you're not doing those things required to achieve spiritual maturity like getting to know God, building a relationship with Him by studying His Word, praying and living a holy life. If you're feeling like nobody loves you, examine yourself. Make sure you're a loving person. If you're feeling lonely, make sure you're taking the proper actions necessary to overcome loneliness like taking opportunities to socialize with other godly people and inviting others who have similar interests as yours into your circle. If you feel like the world is against you, make sure it's not because you're against the world. If you feel like you have no friends, make sure it's not because you're not being friendly. Start making things happen in your life instead of waiting for things to happen. With God's help, you have the power to change your life and your circumstances. If you don't like your life, reinvent it. Make your life over. You may not be able to change everything you're not satisfied with, but work to change the things you can. Start paying close attention to your thoughts, words and actions. Decide that you're not going to make any more excuses for not becoming the person God wants you to be.

As you move toward responsibility and accountability, you will start seeing changes in your life. Your mind and your thoughts will be different. You'll be better equipped to see God's plan for your life. The Bible says, *"Show me Your ways, O Lord. Teach me Your paths"* (Psalm 25:4). God has a path already planned for your life, but you can't see it if you're constantly focusing on others, blaming others, putting responsibility off on someone else, blaming them for where you are, never willing to say, "I'm responsible."

God is holding you responsible for your life. No one else can live for you, and no one else can be held accountable for you. *"For we must all appear before the judgment seat of Christ, that each one may receive the things done in the body, according to what he has done, whether good or bad"* (2 Corinthians 5:10).

FOR DISCUSSION

1. What does it mean to take responsibility for your life?
2. One of the greatest lessons you can learn in life is the fact that no one is responsible for your life but you. What are some of the negative consequences of holding others responsible for misfortune that comes into your life?
3. To take responsibility is to take ownership. With ownership comes cost and sacrifice. What is meant by this statement? Give examples.
4. The Bible gives examples of individuals who didn't cause their misfortune, but didn't rebel against those who did. Read Genesis 29:15-39. Share the details of this story, as well as Jacob's response to the deception that was orchestrated against him. How did he show responsibility?
5. Unfortunately, there are times when someone has to remind us of our responsibility. Read 2 Samuel 12:7-12. What happened here and what were the events surrounding this passage of Scripture?
6. What are some characteristics of people who play the blame game?
7. What does it mean to, "Take lemons and make lemonade?" Share a situation where you were given lemons and had to make lemonade.
8. Take a minute to do a quick self-examination. Looking at the big picture; are you satisfied with where you are in life? If yes, share some of the keys to your contentment.

9. If a sister confides in you and shares that she is totally disappointed with her life and just can't seem to get on the right track, how would you counsel her? What Scriptures would you share with her? See Philippians 4:13, Jeremiah 29:11, and Romans 12:6-8.

10. Read 2 Corinthians 5:10. Discuss this verse of Scripture as it relates to responsibility.

Chapter 16

Know When to Let Go

"Anxious to Get Home"

*"Brethren, I do not count myself to have apprehended;
but one thing I do, forgetting those things which
are behind and reaching forward to those things
which are ahead" (Philippians 3:13).*

"Y'all get up!" That was the sound of my mother screaming for us to wake up, get out of bed and get ready for school. She knew this was the best way to get our attention. When we heard my mother yell, "Yawl get up!" we dared not get out of bed.

My feet hit the floor and I started my normal routine; washed my face, brushed my teeth and started getting dressed for school. I can't remember if I ate breakfast that morning or not. My mom would bake homemade biscuits every morning, which is why breakfast was my favorite meal of the day. She'd make a big pot of sugar syrup to go with them, and we would fill our plates with hot biscuits, sugar syrup and butter.

I remember my dad being home that morning, which was quite unusual due to his busy work schedule. In fact, by the time we got out of bed each morning, he was already off to work.

Just moments before the bus came, my siblings and I headed out the door one after the other. When I got outside, I noticed that our little puppy was running loose. Oh well, I thought. She'll be okay. As I ran to the bus stop, I could see my puppy running behind me. "Go back! Go back!" I yelled as I ran and got on the bus. The bus driver waited for us to find our seats before he allowed the bus to start rolling. When the last person sat down, the bus started down the road. As we rolled on, I looked out the window and could see my puppy running alongside the bus. Then all of a sudden, I heard the screams. The wheels of the bus had hit her. She continued to scream as she ran back toward the house while the bus rolled on down the road.

That was probably the longest, saddest day I can remember as a child. I had to spend the rest of the day at school not knowing how our puppy was doing, not knowing whether she would make it or not. Getting through the day would have been a lot easier had I owned a cell phone like some second-graders do today. I could have called or even sent a text message. But unfortunately, we didn't have cell phones, nor could I e-mail my mom and dad to find out the status. We didn't have computers. My only comforting thought was the fact that my dad was home and would be able to take care of our puppy and hopefully nurse her back to health.

When the bus finally pulled up to our house, Dad was there at the bus stop waiting. I didn't see the puppy, and from the look on Dad's face, I could tell something was wrong.

Unfortunately, our little puppy didn't make it. Dad had buried her before we got home. According to him, she lived only a short while before passing away.

This would be my first real experience of having to let go of something. The scars from that experience are still sensitive, even today. Since then, I've not owned another pet.

The Process of Letting Go

Letting go is the process by which something is released, and the first step in the process is recognizing that something or someone is gone, is no longer working, or is no longer necessary, and holding on could do more harm than good.

The second step in letting go is making a conscious decision to let go, and this quite often is the most challenging and difficult step. Making the decision to let go is a decision that must be made with the heart. However, many times, it's made with the emotions. When you make decisions with your emotions, they almost never become firm, final decisions. You'll find yourself on a roller coaster ride. One day you let go, and the next day you take it back.

The third step in the process of letting go is to release. In this step, you let go of something or someone, a situation or circumstance, recognizing that releasing is necessary, and that God will replace what you released with something greater, something better, something necessary for your journey toward becoming the person He created you to be.

Letting Go of Unhealthy Relationships

Lord, help me let go! Surely, this is a prayer you've prayed at some point in your life. It seems, especially for women, it's not uncommon to struggle with letting go. In fact, it's a woman's nature to hold on to things. If you don't believe this, look in your closet, drawers, pantry and cabinets. If you're like some, you get attached to things and want to hold on to them, even things you no longer need; things you'd actually be better off without.

Consider your experiences in letting go. In what areas of your life have you had challenges? Letting go of a relationship is perhaps something you've experienced. This is not uncommon. Relationships don't always turn out the way we plan. I've seen situations where male and female enter into a relationship certain they're the perfect match for each other, only to learn, that's not the case. Then there's the friendship between two people that lasts for what seems like forever, that is, until one day, some sort of challenge threatens the relationship and tears it apart. Letting go of a relationship isn't always easy, especially when there are emotional ties. You may be emotionally attached and in love with someone, but know this is an unhealthy relationship, a relationship you know you need to release and let go.

There are so many scenarios where women have found themselves in relationships they know they shouldn't be in. There's the relationship where the person you're in love with is a married man. There's the relationship where the person you're in love with has different morals and values than you. There's the relationship with the person who is the same sex as you. There's the relationship with the person who physically abuses you. There's the relationship with the person who uses you, takes advantage of you and doesn't appreciate you. There's the relationship with the person who's always dishonest. There's the relationship with the person who just doesn't want to be with you.

Perhaps you're a married woman and you're struggling with a difficult marriage relationship. If this is the case, letting go doesn't necessarily mean divorce. God hates divorce. *"For the Lord God of Israel says that He hates divorce"* (Malachi 2:16). But letting go can mean seeking help from godly people, such as family members, spiritual counselors and others who care about you and your husband and can assist you in getting help for your marriage. Let go of those things that are hindering you from getting up, getting the help you need and moving your marriage to a place where it's well pleasing to God. Get help for yourself first, then you can get help for your spouse.

Letting Go of Unhealthy Attitudes

Perhaps you hold on to negative attitudes. If this is the case, know that negative attitudes can keep you from moving forward and achieving important goals you've set. If you've struggled with losing weight, before you can turn things around, you have to let go of that attitude that says, "I just can't do it." Perhaps you struggle with always being late. You never get anywhere on time. Well, before you can start getting to places on time, you have to let go of that attitude that says, "I can't get anywhere on time." If you have a problem with drugs or alcohol, you won't be able to change your habits until you let go of that attitude that says, "I just can't quit."

A negative attitude will affect everything about you. Your attitude spills over into every aspect of your life. Have you ever been around a negative person? If you say, "It's a pretty day outside." They say, "So what. I'm sure it'll be raining tomorrow." You say, "I like that dress you're wearing." They say, "This old ugly thing? I got this from a garage sale." You say, "Hey, how was work today?" They say, "I hate my job and all the people who work there." You say, "I baked cookies. You want one?" They say, "You baked them? I don't think so." Do you know this person? Are you this person? Are you the person with the negative attitude, the person who just expects for things to go wrong? Your favorite words are: I can't. I don't want to. I'm not going to. Did you know the attitude you possess could make the difference in the quality of life you enjoy and can even affect your health? Think about it. A person with a negative attitude who expects for things to always go wrong—what do you think would happen if this person were to be diagnosed with a serious illness? This is the person who would be less likely to take their medication properly because they don't think it's going to help them anyway.

Let go of those attitudes that are a hindrance, those that keep you from achieving your goals. It's a lot easier to possess a positive attitude than it is to carry around the weight of a negative attitude.

Letting Go of Anger

One of life's greatest challenges is letting go of anger. Being angry is an emotion that will naturally express itself when something painful happens to trigger the emotion. Anger grows out of pain, and the pain is born most often when you've been wronged or offended by someone. Anger most always leaves you with a desire to retaliate.

Anger is a powerful emotion, and many times difficult to release and let go. There are marriages that might have survived had couples let go of anger. There are friends who might still be friends had they let go of anger. There are churches that might never have split had members let go of anger. There are wars that might never have been fought, had leaders let go of anger. Anger can bring all kinds of destruction, and sometimes, it takes a lifetime to recover.

No person is exempt from getting angry. As long as you live, you will have the capacity to get angry. As long as you interact with people; your spouse, children, relatives, friends, co-workers and others, because of the potential for conflict, the potential to become angry will always be there. You've heard of road rage. There's even the potential for conflict on the roadways, which creates an opportunity for anger to surface. No matter how hard you try, you cannot escape anger.

It's easy to become consumed by anger, and it can happen so fast. Anger is not discretionary. Before you know it, you can find yourself unleashing anger on people closest to you, and usually, when the anger comes, so do the harsh words, and words are like eggs. Once you scramble them, they can't be unscrambled. Once your tongue is used to speak words that are harsh and destructive, those words can't be taken back. *"But no man can tame the tongue. It is an unruly evil, full of deadly poison"* (James 3:8).

Being angry in and of itself is not the problem. However, how you express anger can become a problem if you don't express it in productive ways that lead to peace. *"Be angry, and do not sin. Do not let the sun go down on your wrath"* (Ephesians 4:26).

The most important step in letting go of anger is, deal with the source of anger, and deal with it in the right spirit, with the right words and in the right tone of voice. Use wisdom to effectively deal with the issue at hand, the source of the problem. This would be the mature response to anger, and this takes practice, as well as consciousness and awareness. Anger can become so severe that it blocks all rational behavior. However, as a child of God, the Holy Spirit dwells in you, and when He lives in you, when anger comes, if you allow Him to, the Spirit of the Lord will move you out of the way and allow His Spirit to shine through. This type of reaction comes with spiritual growth and maturity.

Why You Should Let Go

There are several reasons you should let go. First of all, know that there are blessings in store for you, but unless you let go of what's hindering you, you may forfeit the release of those blessings. Until you let go of the old, you have no room for the new.

If I buy new clothes and hang them in my closet year after year, there is going to come a time when I have to get rid of something in order to make room for my new clothes. Does that make sense? If I don't get rid of some of my used clothes; give them to charity, or to someone I know can use them—if I don't do something with them, I'm going to have clothes everywhere and that's going to create a cluttered environment. If I keep stocking my pantry with canned goods week after week, at some point, I'm going to have to get rid of some of those cans. Canned goods have an expiration date. What would happen if I just kept letting my canned goods pile up and never used them, never got rid of them? Pretty soon, I'd have a pantry full of old, expired canned goods that no longer could be used.

"Brethren, I do not count myself to have apprehended; but one thing I do, forgetting those things which are behind and reaching forward to those things which are ahead" (Philippians 3:13). Letting go is a biblical principle. Paul knew the importance of letting go and recognized the role it plays in spiritual growth and development. No doubt he felt compelled to let go and put some things behind him. Perhaps you're being compelled to let go of something. If so, recognize this for what it is. This could very well be the Holy Spirit's presence trying to let you know God has something in store for you, but you can't receive, until you release. There could be places God wants you to go, things He wants you to do and blessings He has in store for you. But until you let go of all that's hindering you; people, thoughts and attitudes, anger, unforgiveness and such, you can never get to the place God wants you to be.

There's another reason letting go is necessary. When you let go, you're basically saying, "Lord, I surrender all to you. I'm depending on you. I trust you." Letting go demonstrates your dependency on God. Suppose you are the parent of a wayward adult child. You've done all you can to help your child. You raised him the best way you knew how. You've helped him get jobs that he didn't keep. You've given him money. You've paid his bills, and every time he goes to jail, you bail him out. He's become such a financial burden until you don't know how your bills are going to get paid. Sometimes it's necessary to let go of a wayward child, as difficult as it may be, and recognize that you're doing him or her more harm than good. Letting go of your child doesn't mean you won't be there when they're ready to repent and become a productive citizen in society and a servant in God's kingdom. But it does mean allowing them to make mistakes, learn from them and endure the consequences of their choices. Most of all, letting go of a wayward child means trusting God to take care of your child once you've released them. As long as you hold on to your child because you're afraid of what might happen to him or her if you let go, you're denying that God can take care of your child.

Another reason you should let go of things that are a hindrance in your life is to give yourself peace of mind. Peace of mind can be described as the absence of mental and emotional stress or anxiety. It can be described as free from worry. To have peace of mind is to be able to sleep at night knowing you've let it go. You don't have that issue or drama in your life anymore. Holding on to something you know you need to let go causes a lot of stress. Admit it. It takes a lot of time, effort and energy. You think about it a lot. You lose your appetite over it. You lose sleep over it. You just can't rest.

Perhaps you've experienced going to work and thinking to yourself, "I can't do another thing until I clean up and organize this desk." Or, even at home, maybe you've walked into your bedroom and said, "I can't do another thing until I clean up this room." The process of cleaning up and cleaning out may not have been all that pleasant, but do you remember the feeling you had when you got it all cleaned up? When the job was finished, do you remember the calmness, the peace you felt?

When you decide to let go and clean out the old to make room for the new, the process will be a challenging one, but in the long run, it'll be well worth it. When all is said and done and you're at peace with yourself, you'll look back and wonder how you held on for so long.

Tools for Letting Go

The Bible encourages seeking wise counsel. It's good to have someone you can talk to and tell your troubles to, someone you can open up and share with during that letting go process. "*A wise man will hear and increase learning, and a man of understanding will attain wise counsel*" (Proverbs 1:5). Seek out a godly person who can share God's Word and take you to the throne of God in prayer.

Secondly, use wisdom. You're going to have to admit that there are just some things you cannot change. You may be good at a lot of things, but there are some things you cannot fix, you cannot make better, and you cannot change, and that certainly applies to other people. Only God can change people.

Finally, God has given us a Helper in life; His Holy Spirit. *"And I will pray the Father, and He will give you another Helper, that He may abide with you forever"* (John 14:16). When God gives you something to do, you can rest assured that He's given you everything you need to get it done. If He's asking you to let go, He's already given you the strength you need to do it by the power of His Holy Spirit.

FOR DISCUSSION

1. What does it mean to let go of something?
2. Letting go is a process. See page 169 and discuss some of the important elements in the process of letting go.
3. It can be especially difficult for children to let go, especially when there's a divorce, loss of a long-time pet, loss of a friend or loss of someone or something else they love. What are some keys to helping children successfully go through the process of letting go?
4. Read Genesis 19:26. What do you think was on the mind of Lot's wife that caused her to look back? Could the inability to let go have caused her to look back? Explain.
5. Many women remain in unhealthy relationships because of the difficulty in letting go. Some situations might require Christian counseling from someone who is skilled in the Scriptures, especially when marriage is involved. Share an experience you've had in letting go of a toxic relationship. What advice would you give to a woman struggling to let go?
6. Toxic relationships aren't the only things we women struggle with letting go of. We also struggle with letting go of things that are simply becoming clutter; old shoes, handbags, sweaters, Tupperware containers, lids that don't fit anything, etc. Have you ever watched the television show Hoarders? Why is it sometimes difficult for us to let go of things we never use anymore? What are some of the clutter items you are holding on to and need to let go?
7. Letting go of the old is necessary to make room for the new. Mentally and emotionally speaking, what does this mean?
8. How does letting go demonstrate our dependency on God? Give Scriptures to support your answer, including Philippians 4:19.
9. Read Genesis 22:9-12. What does this passage of Scripture teach us about letting go? What is a key element in letting go?

10. It's not uncommon to give something over to God, only to take it back again, as though we don't trust God with it. Why is it sometimes difficult to take it to the Lord and leave it there?

Chapter 17

Learn How To Fly

"My First Flight"

*"I can do all things through Christ who
strengthens me" (Philippians 4:13).*

It was my first time flying. I was so excited when my boss told me I would be traveling to Louisville, Kentucky to be trained on our new computer software. I was even given a company credit card to book all of my expenses. That was a big help. I was a single parent at the time and didn't have extra cash to prepay my expenses, especially not a round-trip plane ticket and a week of hotel expenses.

On the morning of my flight, I got up and checked with the airline to make sure my flight was still on schedule, looked out the window to see what the weather was like, got dressed and headed for the airport. Thank goodness my sister was available to look after my son.

I dressed casual because I didn't have any meetings that day. I wasn't scheduled to start training until the following morning. I really wasn't sure what to expect from the plane ride since I had never flown before. I made it to my gate in plenty of time. I had a few extra minutes to browse the terminal and pick up a couple of magazines.

When it was finally my turn to board the plane, I handed the attendant my boarding pass and hurried down the tunnel to the plane.

I sat in the middle of the plane. In fact, I was sitting on the wing. Finally we were backing out and headed for the runway. In just a couple of minutes, the plane was taking off, headed up into the clouds.

Everything was going well and then all of a sudden it felt like the plane was losing its balance. It was shaking and even dropping what seemed like several feet. I was so frightened. I just knew the plane would be going down at any moment. I looked around and all the other passengers seemed calm. It seemed like I was the only one disturbed by the turbulence.

The plane had to stop in Chicago, and it didn't stop shaking and dipping until we landed there. And, the rest of the way to Louisville was no different. By the time I got to my destination, I was a nervous wreck. During my entire stay in Louisville, I tried to figure out how I could get back home some other way than by plane.

When it was time to head back to the airport for the trip home, I dreaded it. I couldn't bear the thought of going through another turbulent flight like the one that brought me there. I boarded the plane and tried to relax. By the time we made it back to our stop in Chicago, I had seriously made up my mind to call my mother and have her drive to Chicago and pick me up.

Needless to say, my first trip on an airplane wasn't a pleasant experience.

Understand the Principles of Flying

Since my first flying experience, I've flown many times. However, I have to say, the emotional trauma of that first flight left a bit of a scar. To this day, I'm not totally comfortable when I get on a plane.

Flying on an airplane is one thing, but soaring in life is another. However, the concepts are similar. There are certain principles that apply to an airplane in order for it to fly, and there are certain principles in life you must follow in order to be able to soar. And just as you'll experience turbulence on an airplane, you'll also experience turbulence when soaring in life.

A life that soars is a life that rises above negative circumstances and situations. It's a life that rises above adversity and disappointments. A life that soars has learned how to win at life, how to overcome and achieve. This person has learned the principles needed to fly and has put those principles into practice.

Perhaps you are a parent. Parents want their children to grow up, leave the nest and fly high into the sky of life. I can remember as a child finding a bird's nest. We lived in the country, so in the summertime, my siblings and I practically lived outside. As we would play outside, hiking in the woods, climbing trees, it wasn't unusual to find a bird's nest nestled behind the branches of a tree with two, maybe even three eggs. In fact, finding a bird's nest was the highlight of many days. When we would find a nest, we'd check it every day to see if the eggs had broken open. In time, we would find tiny baby birds. It was amazing to see this miracle of life. Every day we would go check on the little birds. We watched them as they held their mouths wide open so they could be fed. The mother bird would go out and get food and bring it back to her babies.

It was not uncommon for my siblings and me to find a tiny baby bird on the ground that perhaps had a difficult time catching on to that flying thing. We never saw it happen, but we thought maybe the baby had been pushed out of the nest by the mother bird in her attempt to teach her baby how to fly. I can remember picking a little bird up from the ground, putting it into the cup of my hands and throwing the bird up into the air, hoping it would fly away. But most of the time, it would fall to the ground. Sometimes we would find that a little bird had a broken wing, or was just too weak to fly.

If you're a parent, you've likely watched your child fly out of the nest, taking that leap into society. When they left the nest, your experience was similar to what a mother bird would experience. You did all you could to teach your child the ways of life. You raised them up against a spiritual backdrop, you equipped them with an education and all the tools of life, but still, unfortunately, your child has had a difficult time learning to fly, learning to successfully navigate society. Instead of soaring high above, they just can't seem to be able to catch on.

What about you? What about your life? Someone once pushed you out of the nest. Did you learn to fly? Or, is your situation like the bird I threw up in the air, only to watch it fall to the ground? If this is your situation, know that it's never too late to learn to fly. But flying requires preparation. You can't just expect to jump out of the nest into society without proper flight training. Many persons who have fallen in society have done so because they lacked proper principles of flying. If you are one of those persons having difficulty spreading your wings and learning to soar, you likely have missed grasping the concept of those principles.

Be a Good Listener

In order to be able to fly, to navigate through life, you have to be a good listener. Have you ever flown on an airplane? If so, just like I did, you probably get that bit of nervous tension that's normal when you know you're not in control. When you're flying on an airplane, you want to make sure the pilot flying the plane is a good listener. Thousands of planes fly in and out of airports daily. There is a lot of room for mistakes when airplanes are taking off and landing all day and night. To keep from having accidents, there is a system of communication going on between pilots and what's called, air traffic control. Air traffic controllers give instructions to the pilots. They tell them when it's safe to take off and when it's safe to land. They warn them when there's bad weather ahead. When you're flying on an airplane, you want to make sure the person piloting the plane is a good listener and understands instructions.

Listening is a very important element in the process of communicating, and even more so, when you're confronting difficult issues. It's common to think that such things as having the ability to articulate well and formulate and properly structure a sentence are the most important things in communicating. While those are important in the process, listening is just as important.

A good listener listens not just with their ears, but also with their heart. They hear what's being communicated. How often have you been in a conversation with someone, and instead of truly listening to what they were saying, you were formulating your answer, figuring out what you were going to say when they finished talking? This is an example of poor listening skills.

Does anyone listen anymore? It doesn't seem like it. This was humorously demonstrated at an event I attended. The icebreaker was a listening exercise. Everyone got in a line, and the first person in line was given a message to be carried all the way to the last person in line. The first person whispered the message to the next in line and so on and so on, until the last person received the message. The object of the game was to see how much the message changed from the first person to the last. It was amazing. By the time the message got to the last person, it was a totally different message.

Poor listening habits lead to mistakes, miscommunications and misunderstandings. Suppose I call you on the phone and say, "I'm flying home tomorrow and would like for you to pick me up. My plane comes in at ten o'clock tomorrow night." However, the next morning, you arrive at the airport at ten o'clock because you thought that's what I said. Because you weren't properly listening, you caused yourself a huge inconvenience. You adjusted your work schedule and as it turned out, it wasn't even necessary. I told you ten o'clock at night, not morning. This may seem small, but little things such as this can commonly be the reason for flying failures.

Listening is not just something you do with your ears. As you listen, you should listen attentively with your heart, as well. Many who by now should be soaring to new heights are not because they listened only with their ears. You've heard of "in one ear and out the other." That's what happens when you listen only with your ears. Your parents, friends and others said to you, "Don't marry him. You deserve better." But, it went in one ear and out the other, and now you admit, "I should have listened." Or, perhaps in your young life, you contemplated dropping out of college, and family, friends and others said to you, "Don't drop out of college. You'll regret it in the long run." But, it went in one ear and out the other. You dropped out anyway, and now, you admit, "I should have listened."

There are so many individuals who are walking when they should be flying, should be soaring; all because they didn't listen when someone gave them good, sound advice about life and living. They didn't listen with the heart.

Just Do It

Another principle you will need to follow in learning to fly is a principle called, "Just do it." You're familiar with Nike commercials. Nike branded the slogan, "Just do it." Ask yourself, "What do I want out of life? What do I want the environment of my life to look life? What contribution do I want to make to society?" Well, what's holding you back from spreading your wings and flying, soaring in life, achieving your dreams, getting the most out of life, living the best life you can live? Just do it!

Trust that life contains everything you need to soar. *"Therefore I say to you, do not worry about your life, what you will eat or what you will drink; nor about your body, what you will put on. Is not life more than food and the body more than clothing? Look at the birds of the air, for they neither sow nor reap nor gather into barns; yet your heavenly Father feeds them. Are you not of more value than they"* (Matthew 6:25-26)? Jesus addresses the issue of worry in this passage of scripture. Worrying can certainly keep you from soaring. But know that as you soar, if you stay on the course God has charted for you, there's no need to worry. All of your needs will be met.

The alternative to "Just do it" is, just live a mediocre life, a life where you just exist from day to day, doing just enough to get by, nothing more and nothing less. I believe that as women, as we grow older, our creative awareness and consciousness become stronger. Our ability to create the lives we desire to live becomes stronger. Several years ago, I was having challenges with periods of depression, and I went to a doctor who talked to me about the cycles of life that women go through, and how that as we grow into life, and as we age, we become more creative. I remember him telling me that some of a woman's most creative moments happen later in life. As I've grown older, I've often thought about that conversation even as I've experienced my own moments of creativity. Based on my own experiences, I believe what my doctor said. In a sense, and by the power of God, life has opened up and cooperated with me in meeting many of the goals I've set in life. God has opened doors that at earlier stages in my life seemed as though they would never open. There is a level of creativity that comes with age, but unfortunately, far too many women will fail to use their creativity as a launching pad from which to soar. Or, many will experience an unsuccessful launch, fall down and never get back up. But when you have the attitude that says, "Just do it," even when you fall, you realize where your strength comes from. You realize, God has your back. You pick yourself up, spread your wings and try it again. You've learned the principle that says, "Just do it!"

The principle of "Just do it!" can also be referred to as the principle of persistence. The Bible talks about being persistent. *"Ask, and it will be given to you; seek, and you will find; knock, and it will be opened to you. For everyone who asks receives, and he who seeks finds, and to him who knocks it will be opened"* (Matthew 7:7-8).

A person who is successful at flying is a person who is persistent. Falling is a big disappointment. There's nothing like thinking it's going to happen this time. This is it. I'm going to do it, only to spread your wings and fall down. Such is life. Experiences such as these are common when it comes to flying. But know that sometimes a fall is necessary. God will allow you to fall in order to teach you a lesson or a principle you may need later in your flight. God can see way out ahead of you, way down the path, while you can only see what's in front of you. God is not in the business of allowing disappointments in your life just for the fun of it. You can best believe, when God allows a disappointment, when He allows you to fall, there's a reason behind it. The life you are destined to live, the path that was created for you; God has already designed it. You're simply trying to find the course. If He allows you to do it your way, you may never find the path He wants you to travel. It's human nature for us to choose the path that's quicker, easier, more comfortable and has no turbulence. But that's likely not the path that leads to the life God wants you to live. God's path won't be so quick, easy and comfortable. It will include turbulence, emergency landings, as well as holding patterns.

Wait on the Lord

Learning to patiently wait is a principle that will serve you well as you learn to soar in life. Are you familiar with a holding pattern? This is an air-traffic term. I was on a flight coming home once and was so glad to finally be about to land. When I thought we should have been landing, it seemed that the plane was just sitting there in the air, not really moving much at all, except for a bit of circling every once in a while. Shortly after, the pilot came on the intercom and announced we were in a holding pattern. That meant we couldn't immediately land. All we could do was wait our turn to be given the approval to land.

Have you ever felt like you were just standing still in life, like your life was on hold, like nothing was happening for you? If so, perhaps you were in a holding pattern. When God puts you in a holding pattern, you spend a lot of time waiting. One of the things you may find yourself tempted to do when you're in a holding pattern is jump out in front and take matters into your own hands. This is especially true of a woman with a controlling personality, who is used to being in control and taking matters into her own hands. Remember Sarai in the book of Genesis? Her name was later changed to Sarah. She found herself in a holding pattern, grew tired of waiting and took matters into her own hands.

Sarai was the wife of Abram. His name would later be changed to Abraham. God told Sarai and Abram they would have a son. But because Sarai became impatient when she hadn't conceived, she told her husband to sleep with her maid, Hagar, so he could have a son. Abram agreed. "*So Sarai said to Abram, "See now, the Lord has restrained me from bearing children. Please, go in to my maid; perhaps I shall obtain children by her.' And Abram heeded the voice of Sarai. Then Sarai, Abram's wife, took Hagar her maid, the Egyptian, and gave her to her husband Abram to be his wife, after Abram had dwelt ten years in the land of Canaan. So he went in to Hagar, and she conceived. And when she saw that she had conceived, her mistress became despised in her eyes*" (Genesis 16:2-4).

After Hagar got pregnant, she started treating Sarai harshly. "*Then Sarai said to Abram, "My wrong be upon you! I gave my maid into your embrace; and when she saw that she had conceived, I became despised in her eyes. The Lord judge between you and me'*" (Genesis 16:5). Instead of waiting on the Lord, Sarai tried to fix the situation in her own way. She came up with her own plan of action and found herself in an uncomfortable predicament.

When you find yourself in a holding pattern, don't get ahead of God and try to take matters into your own hands. Be still and wait on the Lord. While you are waiting, spend time in His presence reading and studying His Word. Fast, pray and meditate. That's what God expects you to do when He puts you in a holding pattern. When you get ahead of Him, you interrupt the plan He has for your life. *"For I know the thoughts that I think toward you, says the Lord, thoughts of peace and not of evil, to give you a future and a hope"* (Jeremiah 29:11). God has a reason for putting you in a holding pattern. His reason could be to get your attention, to quiet you, to give you an opportunity to discern His will. When you can do nothing but wait, you are more likely to listen and hear God's instructions for your life.

Know that in time, God will release you from your holding pattern, and when He does, get back up and try again. If you continue to be persistent, no doubt, you will achieve a successful launch. You'll take off, and at first you'll feel some shaking, like you're going to lose your balance. But as you spread your wings of persistence, and as determination takes over, things will begin to smooth out in your flight. And before you know it, you'll feel yourself soaring higher and higher. You'll find yourself achieving your dreams, living a satisfying, fulfilling life, being creative and using your gifts and talents. But something often happens when we begin to soar in life. We forget who supplies the wind beneath our wings. We begin to lose our memory. We forget where our strength really comes from, and we start to think we're flying in our own strength. Just because you've been up in the air for some length of time doesn't mean you're above falling back down to earth. *"Therefore let him who thinks he stands take heed lest he fall"* (I Corinthians 10:12).

When you're soaring high in the sky, be careful lest you lose not only your memory, but also your spiritual vision. When your spiritual vision becomes cloudy, it becomes difficult to see, and you may very well find yourself taking a fall.

You're familiar with the bald eagle. One of the characteristics of an eagle is, they have excellent eyesight. The eagle can see for long distances. In fact, research says their eyesight is five to six times sharper than ours. While an eagle uses its physical vision to stay on course, spiritual vision keeps us on course. When our spiritual vision is sharp, we keep our eyes on the Lord, the One who made it possible for us to fly, the One who is already at our destination.

Then too, sometimes we soar too fast. We get ahead of ourselves. We spread our wings and fly at full speed; gotta achieve this, gotta achieve that, gotta do this, gotta do that, and before we know it, we feel ourselves growing tired, losing our passion for flying, losing energy. The Bible encourages us to be patient. *"But those who wait on the Lord shall renew their strength; they shall mount up with wings like eagles, they shall run and not be weary, they shall walk and not faint"* (Isaiah 40:31). Don't try to achieve everything at once. If you focus on too many things at the same time, you won't do anything well.

Research also says bald eagles are faithful in their relationships. When an eagle pairs with another, they stay together until one of them dies. As you soar, remember that relationships are important in life. Don't always fly solo. It's all right to come down to earth sometimes for the purpose of helping someone else learn how to fly. Don't ever forget the challenges you faced and the turbulence you experienced on your first flight. As you strive to become the person God created you to be, help someone else do the same.

FOR DISCUSSION

1. Have you ever traveled by plane and had a terrible experience with turbulence? Share your experience.

2. There's a form of turbulence that can hinder us from reaching our personal goals and destinations. It can come in the form of losing a job or some other unfortunate circumstance. Name other forms of turbulence that can shake us up. Share a personal experience.

3. Discuss some of the goals you've set in life and achieved, such as earning a college degree, a promotion on the job and other accomplishments. What are some of the goals you would like to achieve, but have not, including how you plan to achieve your goals.

4. It usually doesn't take much to detect a child's gifts and talents. What should a parent do when they begin to notice that a child might be endowed with certain gifts that have the potential to be developed?

5. Read John 10:10b. Is this Scripture referring to an abundance of material wealth and possessions? What does the abundant life that Christ speaks of in this Scripture look like?

6. In our churches and in society in general, we can see a host of phenomenal women using their gifts and talents and making a positive difference. Unfortunately, it's not uncommon for women to compare themselves to others and even develop an unhealthy competition with others. What can be the root causes of this issue? When we begin to feel unhealthy emotions towards other sisters, what's the best way to handle it, keeping in mind, it starts with self. Reference Scriptures: Galatians 5:26, 6:4, and 2 Corinthians 10:12.

7. One of the principles of flying is, "Be a good listener," page 183. What are some key elements of being a good listener?

Describe some common mistakes we make when someone is talking to us?

8. Discuss key elements of the principle that says, "Just do it," page 185.

9. Discuss the principle, "Wait on the Lord," page 188. What is a key element of this principle?

10. You've heard the saying, "He may not come when you want him to, but He's always on time!" Sometimes we get frustrated when God doesn't show up when we want Him to. You may experience a time in your life when you are simply in a holding pattern. In Genesis 16, Sarai found herself in a holding pattern. What did she do and what were her consequences?